Ketogenic Instant Pot Cookbook

The Ultimate Ketogenic Instant Pot Cookbook – Lose Weight Faster Than Ever With Ketogenic Instant Pot Recipes

Table of contents

Introduction

Hello and welcome to the world of the wonderful Instant Pot and the Ketogenic Diet! If you are reading this then you probably have *some* idea of what the Keto diet is...but it can get a bit scientific! In this book, you will find an easy-to-understand breakdown of the Ketogenic diet, how it works, and the great benefits it offers. You will then come to a list of foods you are allowed to eat, and foods with a big black mark through them...these foods are forbidden. Okay, so it's not quite that scary and strict, but there *are* some rules and requirements. Don't fret about what you can cook for your daily meals, because the most exciting part of this book is the recipe section! The recipes are designed especially for the Instant Pot and come with comprehensive instructions to guide you through.

In the first few chapters of the book, all the bases about the Ketogenic diet are covered just enough so you will be equipped with knowledge by the time you get to the fun part...the food.

All of the recipes included are my original recipes which I cook myself on a weekly basis. They are all Ketogenic-approved and will help you on your own Keto journey. Many of the same ingredients are featured in a lot of different recipes, as some foods are just too perfect to leave out! The Instant Pot features in every recipe, using various functions and settings. The Instant Pot is a fantastic kitchen tool, as it allows you to cook a wide range of different foods easily and without fuss.

A bit about me...

I am not a doctor, dietitian or professional chef. However, I have lived the Keto life! By following the Ketogenic diet, I have lost 9kg and have kept it off. You are in safe hands, as I have studied and researched the Ketogenic diet extensively. I have aimed to give you a comprehensive yet simple rundown of the Ketogenic diet and how it works. I have written the information in my own words, based on my understanding and my own experience of this diet. If you require further clarification or more in-depth, scientific information, there are many online resources to check out. There is a list at the end of this book of great online resources to turn to for more guidance and comprehensive information.

Chapter 1: What Is The Ketogenic Diet?

The Ketogenic diet is essentially an extremely low-carb, high-fat, moderate-protein diet, which relies on the managing of these "macronutrients" in order to force the body into "Ketosis" - hence the "KETOgenic" name. Ketosis happens when the body is deprived of glucose (from carbohydrates and sugars), so it must use stored fats and "Ketones" for energy. Ketones are created when the liver converts fat to energy. That is a *very* simplified explanation, but hey, sometimes simple is best!

Quick tip: It's important to remember that just because you are starving your body of glucose, you are NOT actually starving! You can eat plenty of food to keep you full and satisfied, while losing weight and gaining energy at the same time.

Fun fact: The Ketogenic diet was first formulated and named in the 1920's as a method of controlling epilepsy. Scientists figured out that by reducing sugar and carbs, the body's metabolism acted in a way that was very similar to the way it reacts to fasting. Fasting has been used as a therapeutic method for centuries. (As aptly explained by Dr. Ananya Mandal, MD on www.news-medical.net, a great resource for studies and more "science-y stuff").

How to follow the Keto diet:

Tracking your macros with an app

The first thing you should do is jump online and find a reputable Keto calculator, (Ruled.ME has a good one). You will be required to enter in your age, gender, weight, height, activity level, body fat percentage, and your goals (lose or maintain weight). The calculator will then work out all of the information you need in regards to your calorie intake and the breakdown of macronutrients. The calculator will provide you will the exact number of fats, carbs, and proteins you should be eating a day, in grams. For example, here is my calculation based on my personal details:

Calories: 1611
Fats: 142 grams
Protein: 63 grams
Carbs: 20 grams

1620 cal
132 g fat
20 g carbs
88 g protein

Once you have calculated your particular needs, then voila! You now have a clear idea of how to plan your meals. It's a great idea to download an app such as My Fitness Pal, log in your macro goals, then add in all of your foods to make sure they are fitting the correct requirements. It does take a few days to get the hang of it, but it becomes second nature pretty quickly!

Get to know your Keto foods and write out a shopping list

Print out a list of "yes" foods and "no" foods and stick it to your fridge. By having this list handy, you will be able to quickly plan meals and grab snacks without wondering, "Am I allowed this?"

I recommend writing out a full shopping list to take to the supermarket with you for your first Keto shop. By filling your pantry, fridge, and freezer with Keto-friendly foods, your meal planning will be much easier. Below is a sample shopping list. When it comes to fresh veggies such as lettuce and spinach, it's best to buy them as-needed as opposed to buying a whole lot of fresh veggies at once, as you might not get through them all and they'll go to waste. Buy lots of frozen goods such as frozen berries, beans and meat so you can store them away. Yogurt, butter, and cheese last a while so it's safe to stock up on them.

- Olive oil
- Coconut oil
- Butter
- Full-fat cream
- Full-fat, unsweetened Greek yogurt
- Full fat sour cream
- Hard cheese such as cheddar
- Soft cheese such as mozzarella or ricotta
- Lettuce
- Spinach
- Kale
- Tomatoes
- Broccoli
- Cauliflower

- Eggplant
- Cabbage
- Swiss Chard
- Mushrooms
- Frozen raspberries
- Rhubarb
- Avocado
- Cucumber
- Zucchini
- Free range eggs
- Beef mince
- Lamb mince
- Pork mince
- Beef steaks
- Pork chops
- Chicken breast (free range)
- Chicken thigh (free range)
- Pumpkin seeds
- Macadamia nuts
- Pecans
- Flaxseed (whole or meal)

H2O is your friend!

Remember to drink lots of water on the Keto diet, as sometimes the change in nutrients can cause headaches and constipation (more to come on this!), so keeping yourself hydrated can really help. When you wake up, drink a large glass of water straight away. This will rehydrate your body after your sleep and get you in the "water" mindset for the rest of the day. Buy yourself a good-quality drink bottle and aim to fill it up at least 3 times a day.

Get active, get moving...but keep it chill

Exercise is vital when aiming for optimal health, Keto or not! There have been many studies about the dangers of a sedentary lifestyle, and the benefits of regular movement. However, there are a few things to be aware of when you are following the Keto diet, when it comes to exercise. Ketodietapp.com has a great page about "How to Exercise on a Keto Diet" where they basically advise you to stick to short bursts of exercise, or gentle activity such as walking. If you are thinking "great, I will jump on the treadmill and run for an hour each day so I can lose more weight!", think again! Long and arduous cardio sessions will only make you hungry, tired, and craving carbs!

Here's my experience: when I decided that I wanted to lose weight, I started running long distances every couple of days. Sure, I lost a couple of kg's, but my weight loss didn't match the effort of those tiresome runs I was committing myself to. Then I joined a gym and started doing HIIT training and weights...hello muscles and a smaller waist! Along with Keto, the type of exercise I was doing completely changed my body, and I enjoyed the variation so much more than those long, hard runs. You might experience something completely different, as not all bodies are the same, but I thought I would share my experience with you in case it gives you a burst of motivation and support!

Try walking, weight training, HIIT classes (YouTube has lots of at-home fitness videos!), stretches, Yoga, or Pilates. Listen to your body and take regular rest days.

Quick tip: exercise can help to avoid and relieve constipation, which can be a side effect of Keto due to various factors (read on to find out more).

Relax, breathe, and fight the stress!

Stress is one of those tricky beasts that is hard to avoid, but too much of it can really upset your system, and can even ruin your journey to Ketosis. When you become stressed, your body produces and releases a specific stress hormone. When there is a high amount of this "stress hormone" in your system, your blood sugar increases. A bit of stress here and there is fine, but an ongoing experience of anxiety, stress, lack of sleep, and worry can really put your chances of Ketosis to zero. I might add, if your life has taken a really drastic turn and you are completely stressed out, then maybe put the Keto diet in your diary for a later date. The last thing you want to be doing when life is pushing you around is follow a very strict eating plan! However, if everything is going well but you are prone to bouts of stress, then try meditation, breathing techniques, yoga, walking, or *anything* that calms you! This might be watching TV, talking on the phone to a buddy, dancing, painting...whatever works for you.

Macronutrients: "the big 3" - what they are and how they work

The foods we eat are categorized into different "macronutrients" (more casually known as "macros" if you want to freshen-up your food lingo!). The three main macronutrients are carbohydrates, proteins, and fats. If you want to reach Ketosis, then you really need to pay close attention to your macros. Too many carbs and you'll blow your chances, too many proteins and you can really slow the process or stop it all together. The best way of being sure of the macronutrient breakdown in each meal is to log it into a food calculator. My Fitness Pal is a good one because it gives you the total calories as well as the macro percentages.

1. Carbs

Carbohydrates are most commonly recognized as "starchy" foods such as bread, pasta, potatoes, and rice. However, carbohydrates include sugars and sugar-containing foods such as fruit, candy, cakes, alcohol...you name it. When you eat carbs, your body turns them into glucose (blood sugar), which is then used for energy. As soon as the amount of sugar in the blood is raised, your pancreas gets the message to pump out more insulin, so the blood sugar can be processed and moved around the body as energy.

2. Protein

Protein is a tricky macronutrient because it can convert to glucose if too much of it is consumed. If you go over the "moderate" protein guideline, you run the risk of ruining ketosis by giving your body too much glucose to use as energy, therefore it doesn't go ahead and use the stored fat instead. However, moderate amounts of protein are required because your muscles and tissues need protein in order to grow and repair.

3. Fat

Fat is the teacher's pet of the Ketogenic diet. The majority of your daily meals will be made up of fats. This can sometimes be a hard thing to get your head around, because "fat" can often be ruled out as "bad" and something to be avoided. There are 3 main types of fat: Saturated, monounsaturated, and polyunsaturated. Instead of confusing you with a rundown of these 3 fats, I will provide you with this tip instead:

Fats which are "whole" or "from the source" such as eggs, grass-fed meats, heavy cream, butter, fresh fatty fish such as salmon are all healthy sources of fat. Products which have been processed and refined down to a "different" form than how they started are "bad" fats, such as: margarine and vegetable oils (apart from olive oil). If you are unsure if a fatty food is okay or not, just think: is this in a packet with lots of ingredients and scientific words? Has it been processed to the extent where it comes in a different form from where it started? If so, then avoid it. If you can say, "this food hasn't been processed, it is reasonably close to its original form, and the ingredients list is very short", then go ahead and add it to your list.

Have you reached Ketosis yet? How do you find out?

It all depends on how accurate you want to be. You might just want to follow the diet as closely as you can, and enjoy whatever benefits it brings you without being too precise. This is completely fine! If you know that you have kept to your macro guidelines and you haven't diverted from the course, then you will have reached some level of Ketosis. You will know if you've reached Ketosis by these signs:

- Weight loss! If your weight has dropped, then you're on the right track
- Your appetite has shrunk: you don't get ravenous and you stay full for longer
- Your breath and urine smell a little different: this means there are more ketones in your body, as they can have a slightly sweet smell

- You feel alert, bright, energetic, and focused: ketones are a very effective energy source for your brain, so once your body is producing lots of them, your brain revels in this new energy source and functions at optimal level
- Check this article out for more signs http://www.healthline.com/nutrition/10-signs-and-symptoms-of-ketosis#section1.

If you are wanting to be more precise and accurate, then there are products on the market which can help you to confirm your level of Ketosis. One of the easiest and most affordable tests is the urine test. This is just like a pregnancy test; you pee on a small strip and wait for the colour to change. The number of ketones in your urine will determine the colour of the stick. There are also breath testers for the purpose of determining your level of Ketosis. These tests work like a breathalyzer to test alcohol on the breath, but you are testing for Ketones...not wine! Research online and take a look at various reviews and comparisons to find the best method and product for you.

Macro guidelines: "the macro maths"

The general rule is that your daily food should fit within these macro guidelines:

Fats: 75% of your daily calories
Protein: 20% of your daily calories
Carbs: 5% of your daily calories

Your app will calculate all of your macros for you, so all you need to do is make sure that your fats, proteins, and carbs are keeping within their limits.

Your macro requirements do change a bit according to your weight, but this will be taken into consideration when you log your details into the macro calculator you choose to use.

Risks and precautions

This Keto crash course wouldn't be complete without a section outlining the risks and precautions. With *any* diet under the sun, there are certain things to be aware of.

If you are taking regular medications or you have any existing health conditions, it's best to consult your doctor before you embark on your Keto journey. The chances are they will say "go for it!", but they might have a few pointers and tips for your specific health conditions.

Should it be a "forever" diet?

I won't get into the topic of using Ketosis for medical purposes, as I am not a doctor and it's best to go straight to a medical professional in such cases. However, I *can* talk about the Ketogenic diet as a weight loss and general wellbeing fix. Everyone has different opinions, and some people might want to stay on the ketogenic diet for a long period of time, if not forever. From my experience, the Ketogenic diet is a great diet to use in order to lose the weight you want to lose, and to get yourself into good eating habits. But, I don't think it's a long-term, permanent solution. I would recommend following the Ketogenic diet strictly until you reach your goals, and then slowly introduce a bit more carbs into your diet. Sticking to a *low* carb diet with a little more flexibility is a good idea. Personally, I still stay away from refined sugars, simple carbs, processed foods, and anything "white and starchy". However, I do eat most fruits and add a bit of brown rice or wholegrain bread here and there.

Again, this is just my experience, and yours might be different! But I think that having the knowledge that it's not forever can be quite motivating when first embarking on Keto. If you think of it as the first stage of your weight loss journey and your crash-course in healthy, clean eating, then the process will be much more pleasant.

Quick tip: Some people follow the Ketogenic diet a few days a week, and eat small amounts of carbs on the other days. By doing this, they are still reaching low levels of Ketosis without going overboard and becoming overwhelmed by the restrictions. Look into this option if all-week Keto dieting isn't for you!

Side effects of the first foray into the Ketogenic Diet

Because your body has become accustomed to using glucose from carbs as its main energy hit, it will go through a few teething issues when you take the glucose away. Just like those cutting cigarettes or soda can experience withdrawal symptoms, so can those of us who are going cold turkey on carbs! Your body needs to adjust to using a different energy source that what it's used to, so it can take a while for your brain to regain optimum functionality. During your first few days on Keto, you will likely feel a little "off", but after a week you will start to feel back to normal, if not better! Here are some of the most common side effects you might experience:

1. Having to pee a lot

When you first cut carbs, your body uses up all of the glycogen (glucose is called glycogen once it is stored) that has been stashed away for a rainy day in your muscles and your liver. When your body uses this extra glycogen, it also releases water along with it. Basically...losing water = peeing a lot more often than usual.

2. Tiredness

General fatigue and lack of energy can be expected when you first cut the carbs. Your body is still figuring out how to get the energy it used to get, and it takes a while for it to figure it all out! Also, since you are draining your body of water (hence the aforementioned peeing increase), you will be losing minerals and salts which can also contribute to the tiredness. You can take supplements and electrolytes to stock up your mineral stores. Check with the doctor about getting some magnesium and potassium supplements.

3. Foggy brain

Mental clarity is something you can look forward to once your body gets used to being in Ketosis. However, during the first few days, you might experience the opposite. Your brain has to adjust to the new energy source, so it might lag a bit before it gets back to its highly-functional self! Of course, the loss of minerals can contribute to this as well, so pack your plate full of leafy greens (you should be doing this anyway!) to replace all those much-needed goodies.

4. Tummy troubles

This is one of the more unpleasant side-effects. Constipation can be expected because of the loss of fluid and the decrease in dietary fiber if you are used to getting fiber from fruits, breads and grains. Lots of water and vegetables will help with this, and your digestion will soon get back to regularity.

5. Weaker muscles

Don't expect to head to the gym and break your lifting records during the first week of following the Keto diet. Again, this is just while your body figures out its new fat-based energy source. The loss of magnesium and other minerals can also affect your muscles and you might notice some cramping as well as weakness. Your guns will be back to a fighting-fit state after a week or so, so don't stress!

6. Cravings

If you're like me, then you will be familiar with cravings for treats, Keto or not! You might notice that your mind turns to sugary or starchy treats a lot more than usual during the first week or two of your keto diet. Stay strong and have a green tea instead, (I know, a green tea is no match for candy and cakes, but trust me, you won't even *want* that kind of thing after a while). Once your body "forgets" about carbs and sugars, you will forget about them as well (for the most part...we're only human, aren't we?!)

Quick tips: add salt to your food to replace lost salts from all the bathroom trips. Drink LOTS of water to help your bowels get moving. Really pack your meals full of dark green veggies such as spinach and broccoli, your body will thank you for the fiber and minerals. Get lots of rest and sleep, lay off the hardcore workouts, and wait it out.

Chapter 2: Benefits Of The Ketogenic Diet For General Health

You wouldn't cut out an entire macronutrient food group for no good reason! In fact, there are *many* reasons to try the Ketogenic diet. Here are the main benefits you can expect from the Ketogenic diet if you are generally healthy and do not have any medical conditions. If you have any medical conditions, or you're just a bit unsure, see your doctor! They will give you personalized tips and advice according to your health.

Weight loss

Losing weight is a great way to gain energy and reduce your chances of heart disease, type 2 diabetes, and high blood pressure. If you have extra weight to lose, then a strict Ketogenic diet combined with regular exercise is a great way to go. Once you start to see the results on the scales and in the mirror, you will feel fantastic!

Increased energy

I'm sure you can agree with me on this one: life is tiring at the best of times! We don't always have the energy we need in order to live life to the fullest, and our diet can either help or hinder this. Diets which are high in sugar and starches cause our insulin levels to skyrocket due to the heavy bursts of glucose. High levels of insulin cause tiredness and lethargy, often resulting in the craving for an afternoon nap! When you remove sugars and carbs, your insulin levels decrease and level out as your body is deprived of that devilish sugar. Without the constant rising and falling of glucose and insulin, your energy levels stabilize and even rise, as the foods you are eating offer slow-burning energy to keep you feeling full of beans (not literally of course, no beans allowed on keto!).

Reduction of "dangerous" fat

The soft bits of fat which live on our inner thighs and hips (for the ladies mostly) is different to the hard fat which builds up around our organs (this is called visceral fat). The "lady fat" (feel free to use that term if you wish!) is pretty harmless, whereas a lot of visceral fat can put us at risk of heart complications and other diseases such as Type 2 diabetes. The Ketogenic diet helps to eat away at this very stubborn type of fat, which is great news for your longevity and general health.

Increased levels of "friendly" cholesterol

The word "cholesterol" probably makes you cringe and think of clogged arteries and heart attacks, right? Well, there's actually such a thing as GOOD cholesterol, otherwise known as HDL. www.ruled.me has a great explanation of "good cholesterol" which helped me to understand, this is what I took from it; technically, HDL is actually not a cholesterol molecule itself, it's actually a transportation device for cholesterol – a cholesterol taxi driver...if you will! The role of HDL in the body is to carry cholesterol around the body and deliver it to cells when they need it. If there is any excess cholesterol left over, the HDL bundles it up and returns it to the liver to be disposed of. If you don't have enough HDL, then the "bad" cholesterol doesn't get disposed of properly and ends up gathering in your arteries as a sticky, dangerous mess. The Ketogenic Diet can help to increase your levels of HDL, which helps to decrease the risk of heart disease.

Promotes clear skin

Clear, fresh skin is something we all covet, no matter our age or gender. You'll be pleased to know that the Ketogenic diet can really help to clear up blemished or acne-prone skin!

For some people, acne is a result of foods which cause a hike in blood sugar levels (carbs and sugars!). Therefore, by drastically reducing the amount of carbs and sugars in your diet, your blood sugar will remain more stable, and your skin won't have a reason to break out and cause you grief! In fact, it's no secret that diets high in sugar are the worst kinds of diets when it comes to skin clarity. I can testify that my skin *definitely* cleared up because of the Keto lifestyle I was following. In saying this, I'd like to add that blemishes are not your fault, sometimes they are caused by hormonal issues, especially around the "time of the month". If the Keto diet *doesn't* help with your skin, it's a good idea to check in with the doctor so they can assess you for any other underlying issues.

Chapter 3: Foods To Eat And Foods To Avoid

Here's where it gets a bit...restrictive. But don't worry! There are *plenty* of absolutely delicious, nutritious foods you can eat on the Ketogenic diet. The thing is, many of the "forbidden" foods are foods which *everyone* should be limiting. Foods such as candy, cakes, starchy white carbs, and sugary alcohol don't do anyone any favors unless they are eaten only as very occasional treats. I will be honest, it does get a little hard sometimes when ALL you want is some chocolate and a big bready burger! I feel your pain.

The YES foods

Go ahead and add these foods to your daily menu. Foods which should be eaten in small amounts have an *m* next to them, to remind you to use them moderately. You will see that most of the *m* foods are high in protein, such as meat. They must be eaten moderately so the protein percentage stays within the recommended intake suggested by your macro calculator.

- Leafy green vegetables: Lettuce (all kinds), spinach, Swiss chard, kale
- Asian greens: bok choi, pak choi, Shanghai
- Berries: stick to raspberries and blackberries *m*
- Avocados

- Eggs *m*
- Butter and cream (preferably grass-fed, if possible)
- Coconut oil
- Olive oil
- Avocado oil
- Grass-fed red meats *m*
- Chicken *m*
- Fatty fish: salmon, tuna *m*
- Herbs and spices *m*
- Nuts and seeds such as macadamia nuts and pumpkin seeds

The HECK NO foods: eat none...seriously

These foods are strictly out of bounds:

- **All grains: wheat, oats, quinoa, cereals, bread**
- Starchy vegetables: potatoes, yams, sweet potatoes
- Most fruits: bananas, apples, citrus, pears, peaches, nectarines
- Sugar: maple syrup, honey, basically anything with sugar
- Juice: all kinds as most juices come from sugary fruits
- Beans and legumes: this includes all beans, chickpeas and lentils
- Alcohol: most alcoholic beverages are full of sugar, so they are a big no-no (small amounts of dry wine in cooking is okay)
- Condiments and sauces: most bought sauces are high in sugars and carbs, so it's best to make your own out of simple, whole ingredients such as olive oil and vinegar

Chapter 4: What Is The Instant Pot?

If you don't already own an Instant Pot, you're probably desperate to know what it is!

Okay, so you've heard of a pressure cooker, right? The Instant Pot is a very sophisticated, user-friendly pressure cooker. Unlike stovetop pressure cookers which must be placed over direct heat in order to use, the Instant Pot is an electric cooker. The Instant Pot is a great addition to your kitchen, as it can sit neatly on the bench, ready to be used whenever you require it.

The Instant Pot range of cookers is all classified as "3rd generation cookers" (according to the Instant Pot official website). This means that they are all equipped with special "Smart Programming" technology, which allows you to perfectly cook a range of different foods and dishes.

There are 5 Instant Pot models to choose from: Lux, Duo, Duo Plus, Smart, and Ultra.

All of the models have these functions:

- Sauté and reduce
- Slow cook
- Steam
- Cook rice
- Keep food warm

All models except the Lux 6-in-1 make yogurt. The Smart model has exclusive functions such as the "script" function which allows the user to add or download recipe scripts, which the Instant Pot automatically changes settings according to the script instructions. All of the models are versatile, user-friendly, and can perform a wide range of cooking functions.

Why use it?

There are so many reasons to invest in an Instant Pot, here are some of the great benefits of this genius piece of equipment:

Multitasking = less bulky equipment!

The Instant Pot takes on the task of many kitchen duties including; cooking rice, steaming, sautéing, warming, slow cooking, pressure cooking, making yogurt. Instead of having a separate machine to do all of these jobs for you, the Instant Pot takes care of the job with one machine.

Easy to use, easy to clean

All it takes is a couple of preparatory steps and the press of a button for you to have a delicious meal ready when you want it. To clean, just remove the stainless steel inner pot and give it a scrub!

Allows you to walk away and get on with life without being stuck in the kitchen

Being chained to the stove just so you can enjoy a tender stew or soup for dinner is no fun! And it's not necessary with the Instant Pot. You simply press the button, walk away, and return when the Instant Pot finishes cooking. When using the sauté button, you do need to attend it, as it acts just like a normal pot, but sautéing is usually a quick task anyway.

Pressure cooking with the Instant Pot is fast and safe

Pressure cookers take the tedium out of certain dishes. In simple terms, the Instant Pot uses pressure and heat to cook food quickly, thoroughly, and with much less energy used than traditional cooking methods. The Instant Pot depressurizes and releases steam safely, either manually or automatically.

Pressure cooking with the Instant Pot keeps your food nutritious and healthy

Because of the speed and pressure of the heat inside the Instant Pot, you don't need to use a lot of water. You just need to add enough water to create steam, but a little bit does the trick. Cooking vegetables in a lot of water can extract and waste the nutrients that you want to keep *inside* the food. The Instant Pot keeps all of the goodies inside your food, so they end up in your body, not down the sink!

Pressure cooking with the Instant Pot gets rid of nasty bacteria and viruses

The Instant Pot pressure cooking function heats food to a VERY high temperature, (even hotter than boiling point), which kills all micro-organisms in your foods, including viruses and bacteria. (Check out the Instant Pot benefits page on their website for more info about this!). The DUO Plus, and the Ultra even have a "sterilizing" function.

Chapter 5: Instant Pot Masterclass – A Guide To The Instant Pot Functions

Obviously, when you first get your Instant Pot, make sure to carefully read the instruction manual to get yourself familiar with your amazing new appliance. But if you need a refresher course, (or the manual has gone missing and you just can't be bothered searching!) here are some simple pointers. Oh, I should add, all of these tips apply to all Instant Pot models!

- The "adjust" button is the button to press when you want to change the temperature and time settings by using the plus and minus buttons
- You can also press the "manual" button which also lets you adjust pressure and time
- On Instant Pot versions which feature the "less, normal, more" sign, this refers to temperature and timing, so you can use the "adjust" button to increase or decrease the temperature to the default setting (normal), the highest setting (more), or the lowest (less)

The Instant Pot is *very* simple to use, but here are some simplified instructions and tips on how to use each button:

Soup: the default cook time for the "soup" function is 30 minutes. You can "adjust" the time to 40 minutes, or 20 minutes. This function uses high pressure.

Meat/Stew: the default cook time for the "meat/stew" function is 35 minutes. You can "adjust" the time to 45 minutes, or 20 minutes. This function uses high pressure.

Yogurt: this function allows you to make yogurt in a bowl or jars. This function is almost entirely automatic, but you can "adjust" the time if you wish.

Bean/Chili: the default cook time for the "bean/chili" function is 30 minutes. You can "adjust" the time to 40 minutes, or 25 minutes. This function uses high pressure.

Poultry: the default cook time for the "poultry" function is 15 minutes. You can "adjust" the time to 30 minutes, or 5 minutes. This function uses high pressure.

Rice: this function cooks rice all on its own. Just press the "rice" button and let it do its thing. This function uses low pressure.

Steam: the default cook time for the "steam" function is 10 minutes. You can "adjust" the time to 15 minutes, or 3 minutes. You need to use a steaming basket or rack with this function, because you don't want the food to touch the water at the bottom of the pot.

Slow Cook: the default time for the "slow cooker" function is 4 hours. You can "adjust" the time to the time of your choice. You can "adjust" the temperature to low, normal, or high.

Sauté: this is an incredibly versatile button, as it allows you to use your Instant Pot as a regular pot, for frying, reducing, searing, and sautéing. Press the "sauté" button and "adjust" the temperature to less, normal, or more. Never use the lid when using the "sauté" function.

Keep warm/cancel: this button turns the pot on and off, and to cancel a cooking function if you've pressed the wrong button. If you have a Smart model, this button can be used to keep food warm.

Timer: this button is for when you want your dish to begin cooking at a certain time. Select the function you want to use, then "adjust" to set the time you wish.

Pressure: this button changes the pressure from high to low.

Manual: this button allows you to change the cook time to your preference.

Quick tips:

- Never use the lid when using the "sauté" function.
- When using the "slow cook" function, make sure the steam handle is to either side of the vent, (not in the center, covering the vent).
- Press the "manual" button when you want to set a specific cook time.

Chapter 6: Recipes

Some tips and notes about these recipes

All of these recipes can be entirely or partly made in your Instant Pot. The servings per recipe are specified at the start of each recipe, and you can divide or multiply them according to how many people you are feeding. Many of these recipes utilize the "sauté" function, as the simplicity of these recipes only requires a short amount of cooking. However, you will definitely find plenty of opportunities to use other functions such as "steam", "soup", and "meat/stew". Just remember that sometimes the Instant Pot can take a while to preheat, so it might be best to press the required function button before you start, if you don't want to wait for the pot to heat in the middle of the recipe process. If a direction has quotation marks around it, such as "adjust", this means that the recipe is referring to a specific button which you can locate on your Instant Pot.

These recipes will work in ALL Instant Pots, but if your Instant Pot model has slightly different functions or buttons, just use your knowledge of your pot and use the appropriate buttons. For example, if your pot doesn't have the "more, normal, less" window, then just keep the temperature at its default setting if the recipe says to adjust to "normal". If the recipe says to adjust to "more" or "less", then adjust the temperature on your pot to the higher or lower temperature options.

These recipes follow the Keto rules very strictly. This is because it's much easier for you to reach Ketosis and to feel confident that you are eating the right foods if your recipes don't give you the option to add *bad* foods! Some recipes have ingredients which must be eaten sparingly, as sprinkles or light flavourings such as nuts and seeds, so stick closely to the measurements provided.

I have added a range of modified "classics" such as "Keto carbonara" which gives you that hit of decadent creaminess to satisfy your cravings, without pushing you into non-Keto territory. The "Sides" section is handy, as it is full of great ideas for adding more veggies to your meals as add-ons and side dishes. By upping your non-starchy, low-carb veggie intake you can add more nutrients and bulk out your meals.

Ready to cook? Read on!

Breakfast

A delicious and filling breakfast is definitely something worth waking up for!

These breakfast recipes are simple, easy to put together, and completely Keto-friendly. Most of these recipes utilize the "sauté" function on your Instant Pot. I have provided some easy, quick, and on-the-go breakfast recipes such as "Greek yogurt with nutty-seed sprinkle and berry dollop". You will also find some recipes suited to special occasions or relaxed Sunday morning brunches when you've got a bit more time on your hands, such as "Courgette fritters with smoked salmon and herb yogurt".

Instant Pot Greek yogurt

All Instant Pot models except the Lux 6-in-1 feature a yogurt function. Many of the recipes in this book utilize Greek yogurt, so it's a good idea to make a big batch of it and have it readily available!

Serves: 1 tub of Greek yogurt (about 10 serves)

Ingredients:
- 2 liters full-fat milk
- 2 tbsp probiotic yogurt (make sure the packet indicates that it contains live cultures)

Method:

1. Make sure your Instant Pot is really clean.
2. Pour the milk into the pot.
3. Press the "yogurt" button and "adjust" until it changes to "boil" on the digital window.
4. Secure the lid onto the pot and wait for it to boil the milk.
5. Once the pot beeps, open the lid and wait for the milk to cool down to 115 degrees (you'll need a thermometer for this!).
6. Mix your store-bought yogurt with a little bit of the hot milk, so the yogurt can become smooth and mix in with the milk properly.
7. Pour the yogurt mixture back into the pot and stir into the milk.
8. Replace the lid, press "yogurt", then "adjust" the time to 8 hours.

9. Once the timer beeps after 8 hours, open the lid, take out the yogurt and place it into a cheesecloth sitting in a sieve, over a bowl. This will allow the whey to separate, and leave you with thick, creamy yogurt! Leave the yogurt to strain until it's the thickness you are looking for.
10. Keep in the fridge.
11. ENJOY!

Grated carrot, zucchini, and goat cheese hash

Even though carrot is a "moderate" Keto food, this hash is Keto-friendly because it only has a small amount of carrot. The goat cheese offers a creamy, tangy hit of fatty deliciousness! If you're not familiar with a "hash", it's basically a big mash-up of delicious things, fried and thrown onto a plate to be devoured.

Serves: 4

Ingredients:

- 2 carrots, grated
- 4 zucchinis, grated
- 150gm goat cheese, cut or crumbled into small pieces
- 1 egg, lightly beaten
- 2tbsp olive oil
- 2tbsp fresh parsley, finely chopped
- Salt and pepper

Method:

1. Mix the carrot, zucchini, egg, goat cheese, salt, and pepper in large bowl.
2. Press the "sauté" button on your Instant Pot and drizzle the oil into the pot.
3. Once the oil is hot, tip the vegetable mixture into the pot and press it down almost like a large frittata.
4. Let the mixture fry in the oil for a few minutes, then roughly turn it over, (it doesn't need to turn over in one piece, you can turn it over in multiple pieces), cook the other side for about 3 minutes.

5. Once both sides have turned golden brown and crispy, remove from the pot and serve on plates with any low-carb condiments you like! Homemade mayonnaise pairs really well with this dish.
6. ENJOY!

Salmon and cream cheese on Portobello mushroom "bagels"

Salmon and cream cheese is one of my favourite breakfast combinations, especially on the weekend. The Portobello mushroom "bagels" are a great substitute for those chewy, carb-loaded bread-rings we love to hate! (I'm joking, no carb-hate here...just a carb ban!)

Serves: 4

Ingredients:

- 100gm smoked salmon
- 250gm full-fat cream cheese
- 4 Portobello mushrooms
- 2tbsp olive oil
- Salt and pepper

Method:

1. Drizzle the mushrooms with olive oil and rub a sprinkling of salt and pepper into them.
2. Press the "sauté" button on your instant pot and drizzle some olive oil into the pot.
3. Once the oil is hot, place the mushrooms into the pot and cook each side for about 2 minutes a side.
4. Remove the mushrooms and let them cool a little bit (so the cream cheese doesn't melt!).
5. Smear a generous amount of cream cheese onto each mushroom and top it with the smoked salmon and a sprinkling of pepper (the salmon is already salty so I don't add more salt to mine).
6. ENJOY!

Instant Pot boiled eggs with paprika sprinkle (for busy mornings!)

I know, this is a super simple recipe, and not exactly a dish...but some mornings call for a grab-and-go breakfast! Boiled eggs are a great option as they are low-carb and filling enough to get you to your next meal.

Serves: make as many eggs as you like!

Ingredients:

- Eggs
- Salt
- Paprika
- Water

Method:

1. Pour about a cup of water into the Instant Pot.
2. Place as many eggs as you like into your steaming basket (which came with your Instant Pot) and place it into the pot (resting on the inner edges of the pot so that the pot isn't sitting in the water).
3. Secure the lid onto the pot and press "steam".
4. "Adjust" the time to 5 minutes.
5. Once the pot beeps, leave it to cool down and depressurize on its own.
6. Remove the lid, take out your eggs, rest of them in cold water for an hour.
7. Peel the eggs and sprinkle them with salt and paprika before you eat them.
8. ENJOY!

Steamed veggies with coconut oil drizzle and bacon

Although olive oil is my favourite oil to use, I also LOVE coconut oil. The subtle coconut taste really enhances the vegetables in this dish, while the bacon provides a gorgeous saltiness. This is a great breakfast for when you want to make sure you're getting enough veggies into your daily diet.

Serves: 4

Ingredients:

- 2tbsp coconut oil, melted
- 1 carrot, thinly sliced
- 2 zucchinis, thinly sliced
- 2 big handfuls of baby spinach
- 1 cup button mushrooms, sliced
- 1 cup red cabbage, shredded
- 4 rashers streaky bacon, grilled in the oven and cut into small pieces

Method:

1. Place all of the vegetables into your steaming basket, sprinkle them with salt, and place the basket in the Instant Pot.
2. Pour 1 cup of water into the pot.
3. Press the "steam" button and "adjust" the time for 2 minutes
4. Secure the lid onto the pot.
5. Once the pot beeps, release the steam vent and remove the vegetables.
6. Pour the melted coconut oil over the vegetables and serve with the grilled bacon pieces sprinkled on top.
7. ENJOY!

Goat cheese, sausage, and kale fry-up

Goat cheese makes another star appearance! I can't help it, it's just too good! This time, the goat cheese is partnered with sausage (yum!) and kale. The term "fry-up" just refers to a roughly fried mixture of ingredients.

Serves: 4

Ingredients:

- 150gm goat cheese, crumbled into pieces
- 3-4 low-carb sausages, I like lamb and rosemary, but choose the ones you like!
- 4 cups kale, thinly sliced
- 2tbsp olive oil

Method:

1. Cut the sausages into 1inch pieces.
2. Press the "sauté" button on your Instant Pot and keep the temperature at "normal".
3. Pour the olive oil into the pot.
4. Once the olive oil is hot, add the sausages and sauté until browned.
5. Add the kale and stir until coated in oil, cook until wilted and soft.
6. Remove the sausage and kale mixture and place onto serving plates.
7. Sprinkle the crumbled goat cheese on top.
8. Drizzle a little extra olive oil over the top of the dish and sprinkle with salt and pepper.
9. ENJOY!

Bacon and egg omelette

This is a great recipe for when you feel like something a little bit decadent, but without ruining your Keto efforts. Perhaps this could be your go-to Sunday morning breakfast? Add a side of sautéed mushrooms in butter, or a couple of avocado slices, drizzled with olive oil. Adjust the quantities according to how many people you are feeding. If it's just you, then 2 eggs and 2 rashers of bacon should be fine.

Instant Pot tip: remember not to use the lid when using the sauté function, simply use the pot as you would use any other pot! Press the "sauté" button and adjust the temperature.

Serves: 4

Ingredients:

- 5 free range eggs
- 5 rashers of streaky bacon, chopped into 1cm pieces
- 1tbsp fresh parsley, chopped
- Olive or coconut oil to drizzle
- Salt and pepper

Method:

1. Lightly beat the eggs in a bowl with a fork. Add a pinch of salt and pepper and combine.
2. Press the "Sauté" button on your Instant Pot and keep the temperature at "normal".
3. Add the oil.

4. Once the oil is hot, add the pieces of bacon. Sauté until they are cooked and slightly crispy, approximately 5 minutes.
5. Add the mixed eggs and stir into the bacon.
6. Leave the eggs for 2 minutes or until they are cooked to your liking.
7. Remove the eggs from the pot by removing as a whole omelette, or in pieces to your liking.
8. Sprinkle with chopped parsley.
9. ENJOY!

Mushroom, spinach and cheese "throw together" dish

Cheese? Yes. Mushrooms? Yes. Spinach? YES! Oh, and this one has eggs too, to bind it all together. This is a great dish for when you feel like something Keto-friendly, yet easy, yet a bit decadent. You don't need to worry about being tidy or precise with this one, just throw it all together and enjoy! The Sauté button comes in handy again with this recipe.

Serves: 2 (adjust according to your numbers)

Ingredients:

- 2 eggs
- 2 big handfuls of baby spinach
- 3 large Portobello mushrooms, or a handful of small white mushrooms, sliced
- ½ a cup cheddar or mozzarella, grated
- A drizzle of olive oil
- Salt and pepper

Method:

1. Lightly beat the eggs in a small bowl.
2. Press the "Sauté" button on your Instant Pot and keep the temperature at "normal".
3. Drizzle some olive oil into the Instant Pot and heat till warm but not spitting.
4. Add the spinach and stir into the warm olive oil until wilted.
5. Add the sliced mushrooms and Sauté until soft and browned.

6. Add the eggs and scramble together with the vegetables until almost cooked.

7. Add the cheese and heat through until just melted and the eggs are cooked to your liking (some like their eggs to be more set than others, so it's up to you).

8. Turn off the Instant Pot and sprinkle the fry-up with salt and pepper.

9. Dole out your delicious fry-up and enjoy!

Greek yogurt with nutty-seed sprinkle and berry dollop

While berries should be eaten sparingly on the Keto diet, they are definitely worth adding in. Raspberries and strawberries provide a hit of sweetness and are full of nutrients. The berries really don't need a lot of cooking, as you just want them to reach a thick, dollop-able texture, so the Sauté function is ideal. The nutty-seed mix adds a nice crunch and a hit of good fats. You can toast the nutty-seed mix if you prefer a toasted flavour, simply spread them onto a paper-lined tray and bake in the oven for approximately 10 minutes at 180 degrees Celsius (355f).

Serves: Berry mixture makes one medium-sized jar, or approximately 1 cup of berry mixture.
Nutty-seed sprinkle makes 1 cup of sprinkle – keep it in an airtight container or jar.

Ingredients:

- 1 cup frozen raspberries (fresh if available)
- 1 cup frozen strawberries (fresh if available), chopped
- ¾ cup mixed pecans, walnuts, almonds, macadamias, chopped
- ¼ cup mixed pumpkin seeds, sesame seeds, flaxseeds
- ½ cup unsweetened full-fat Greek Yogurt per person, per serving

Method:

1. Press the "Sauté" button on your Instant Pot and adjust the temperature to "low".

2. Add the berries and about 3 tablespoons of water.
3. Stir the berries in the pot and mash them up with your spoon to release the juices.
4. While the berries are reducing, mix together the nuts and seeds and put them in an airtight container (if toasting, toast them while the berries cook). Keep an eye.
5. Once the berries have reduced to a thick, glossy, jam-like consistency, leave them to cool for about 10 minutes before.
6. Spoon the berries out of the pot and straight into a jar or container.
7. Place your Greek Yogurt into bowls and top with a tablespoon of berry mix, and 2 teaspoons of nutty-seed sprinkle.
8. Grab a spoon.
9. ENJOY!

Zucchini fritters with smoked salmon and herb yogurt

Zucchinis are a fantastic, low-carb vegetable. They are so versatile and offer a great hit of nutrients in many different forms. This particular recipe takes the form of a light, tasty fritter which you can make using the "Sauté" function on your Instant Pot (as you can see already, a very handy function!). Serving the fritters with smoked salmon makes for a delicious, omega-3 filled breakfast or brunch. For the yogurt dip, use any fresh herbs you have!

Serves: approximately 12 small-medium fritters

Ingredients:

- 3 cups courgettes (approximately 4 medium courgettes), grated
- 2 eggs, lightly beaten
- 1tbsp chopped chives or spring onions
- Salt and pepper
- Butter for frying
- 25gm smoked salmon per serving (you can use smoked fillets, or gravlax)
- 1 cup unsweetened full-fat Greek yogurt
- 2tbsp chopped fresh herbs

Method:

1. Prepare the yogurt dip by mixing the yogurt and herbs together in a bowl – done!
2. Mix the grated courgette, beaten eggs, salt, pepper, and chopped chives or spring onions in a bowl.

3. Press the "sauté" button on your Instant Pot and keep temperature at "normal".
4. Add the butter to the pot and heat until melted.
5. Place spoonful of courgette mixture into the bottom of the pot, careful not to overcrowd, approximately 4 at a time.
6. Cook for 2 minutes; turn over, then cook the other side for another 2 minutes.
7. Continue to cook spoonful of mixture until all the fritters have been cooked.
8. Store cooked fritters on a plate with a tea towel over top to keep the heat it.
9. Place 4 fritters on a plate (or more, if you're super hungry!).
10. Place salmon on top of the fritters and a dollop of herb yogurt on the side.
11. ENJOY!

Chia seed breakfast pudding with strawberry rhubarb dollop

If you've never eaten Chia seeds, then definitely give this recipe a go! Chia seeds are a great source of fibre and they are really versatile. They must be rehydrated before eating, as they expand to a gel-like texture, (sounds odd, but trust me, they're delicious). The strawberry rhubarb dollop is similar to the berry dollop in an earlier recipe, but offers the earthy tang of rhubarb. You can store away a jar of strawberry rhubarb dollop in the fridge with your berry mixture, so you can mix and match as you please. I personally don't use any sweeteners, but you can add a few drops of liquid Stevia if you like a sweeter breakfast.

Serves: this recipe is for 1 chia pudding, but the strawberry rhubarb dollop makes approximately 2 cups

Ingredients:

- 2tbsp chia seeds
- ½ cup almond or coconut milk – unsweetened
- Pinch of cinnamon
- 2 cups chopped fresh rhubarb
- A handful of strawberries, chopped (about 8 medium strawberries)

Method:

1. Press the "Sauté" button on your Instant Pot (I promise, the other functions will be used later in the recipe section!) and keep the temperature at "normal".

2. Place the rhubarb and strawberries in the pot with a few tablespoons of water. Mash the strawberries with a spoon to release juices.
3. Sauté the fruit mixture until it is soupy and soft.
4. Turn the pot off and leave the mixture to cool slightly.
5. Transfer the fruit mixture to a jar or airtight container.
6. In a small serving bowl, mix the chia seeds, milk, and cinnamon, cover, and place in the fridge for at least 30 minutes.
7. Once the chia seeds have hydrated, place a dollop of fruit mixture on top (about a tablespoon).
8. ENJOY!

Eggs with asparagus "soldiers"

Did your Mum (or Mom, depending on where you are!) used to make you eggs and soldiers when you were little? Mine did. If you're not familiar, the eggs are soft boiled so the yolk is still runny, and buttered toast is cut into strips – like soldiers! You dip the soldiers into the egg, then eat the hard egg white with a spoon when the yolk is all gone. But of course, because this is Keto, there's NO bread allowed! Instead, the soldiers come in the form of nutritious, delicious asparagus.

Serves: 4

Ingredients:

- 4 asparagus spears per person
- 1 egg per person (or more, if you wish), room temperature
- A knob of butter (approximately a tablespoon)
- Salt and pepper

Method:

1. Press the "Sauté" button on your instant pot and keep the temperature at "normal".
2. Add butter to the Instant Pot and heat until melted.
3. Add the asparagus and sauté until cooked, yet slightly crunchy.
4. While the asparagus spears are cooking, bring a pot of water to the boil.
5. Add eggs to boiling water using a long spoon, and set the timer for 2 minutes.

6. Once the timer rings, remove the eggs and put each one on a plate, in an egg cup if you have one handy!

7. Place asparagus spears on the plate next to the egg, with a sprinkle of salt and pepper.

8. Crack the top off the egg, dip the soldier into the yolk and...

9. ENJOY!

Chorizo sausage with spinach, feta, and spicy tomatoes

Chorizo is one of those satisfying, salty, delicious ingredients and it goes so well with tomatoes. The feta adds a hit of extra saltiness and creaminess, and the spinach packs a hit of those crucial green nutrients! This is another one of those delightfully "casual" dishes that works best when it's thrown together rustically on the plate, to be devoured.

Serves: 4

Ingredients:

- 250gm chorizo sausage, cut into 1 cm chunks
- 4 large tomatoes, any kind works
- Olive oil to drizzle over tomatoes
- 1tsp chilli flakes, (or chopped fresh red chilli if you have it on hand)
- 150gm feta cheese, cut into small cubes
- A few big handfuls of baby spinach, (as much as you like, it wilts with the heat so go for it!)

Method:

1. Turn the oven onto grill, HI temperature.
2. Cut the tomatoes in half and drizzle with olive oil, salt, pepper, and chilli.
3. Press the "Sauté" button on your Instant Pot and "adjust" the temperature by pressing the "+" sign, until the light flashes on the "More" window.
4. Add the chorizo sausage to the pot and stir as it sizzles and releases its oils.

5. Once the oven is heated, place the tomatoes on the rack on the upper half of the oven.
6. Once the chorizo oil has oozed out and the sausage is browning, add the spinach and feta, stir to combine and cover with oils and the spinach is wilted.
7. Once the tomatoes are browned and soft, remove them from the oven.
8. Turn the Instant Pot off and serve the chorizo mixture onto 4 plates.
9. Place 2 tomato halves on each plate.
10. ENJOY!

Soups and Stews (now we get to use another Instant Pot function!)

Soups and stews are a fantastic way to fill yourself up with health-giving nutrients, especially during colder months. The Instant Pot makes stews and soups a breeze to create! Get ready to use those "soup" and "meat/stew" buttons and give the "sauté" button a bit of a break. When using red meat or pork for slow cooked stews and soups, opt for the cheaper cuts, as they are most often the best cuts for these kinds of recipes. Ask your butcher for the best cut of meat for the recipe you are cooking, and they'll know what's best. For example, with slow-cooked or pressure-cooked beef recipes, chuck steak is the ideal choice. (Check out http://www.seriouseats.com/2016/01/best-cut-beef-stew-braise.html for more great info!)

Asparagus soup

Asparagus soup is surprisingly delicious! I love to make this when asparagus is in season. If you're cooking to impress, serve with some grilled bacon on top! Remember to cut off the tough "woody" ends of the asparagus, so you're only using the fresh, green part of the spear.

Serves: approximately 6

Ingredients:

- 1 ½ pounds asparagus, roughly cut into pieces
- 1 small onion, diced
- 2 garlic cloves, finely chopped
- 2tbsp olive oil
- 500ml chicken stock
- 200ml full-fat cream

Method:

1. Press the "sauté" button on your Instant Pot and keep the temperature at "normal".
2. Pour the olive oil into the pot.
3. Once the oil is hot, add the onion, garlic, and asparagus, sauté until the onion is soft.
4. Pour the stock and cream into the pot.
5. Secure the lid onto the pot and make sure the steam valve is closed.
6. Press the "soup" button and "adjust" the time to 20 minutes.
7. Allow the pot to depressurize and cool down on its own.
8. Remove the lid, give the soup a stir, and ladle into serving bowls.
9. Serve with swirl of cream, and a sprinkling of cracked black pepper.
10. ENJOY!

Chicken, white wine, cream and tarragon stew

As far as stews go, this is a very sophisticated and dinner party-worthy recipe! Chicken thighs, cream, white wine, and tarragon are a heavenly mixture. Serve with any low-carb green vegetables you like!

Serves: approximately 6

Ingredients:

- 6 chicken boneless chicken thighs
- 2 garlic cloves, finely chopped
- 1 small onion, finely chopped
- Salt and pepper
- 250ml dry white wine
- 250ml heavy cream
- 500ml chicken stock
- 2tbsp fresh tarragon, finely chopped

Method:

1. Press the "sauté" button and keep the temperature at "normal"
2. Drizzle the olive oil into the pot.
3. Once the oil is hot, add the garlic and onion, sauté until soft.
4. Add the chicken thighs and brown on either side for about 1 minute each, to seal.
5. Sprinkle the chicken with salt and pepper.
6. Pour the wine, cream, tarragon, and stock into the pot and stir to combine.

7. Secure the lid onto the pot and make sure the steam valve is closed.
8. Press the "meat/stew" button and "adjust" the timer to 25 minutes.
9. Once the Instant Pot beeps, allow the pot to depressurize on its own.
10. Remove the lid and serve the stew while it's hot.
11. ENJOY!

Steak and chicken liver stew

Don't be scared by the mention of liver! Liver is such a tasty and nutrient-rich ingredient. Chicken livers, steak, rich gravy, and a hint of garlic...what's not to love!? Go on, be brave and give something new a try!

Serves: approximately 6

Ingredients:

- 1 ½ lb chuck steak (or any other stewing beef you like best), cubed
- ½ lb chicken livers, cut into small pieces
- Salt and pepper
- 1 onion, diced
- 2 garlic cloves, finely chopped
- 2tbsp olive oil
- 1 litre beef stock

Method:

1. Press the "sauté" button on your instant pot and keep the temperature at "normal".
2. Add the olive oil to the pot.
3. Once the oil is hot, add the onion, garlic, livers, and steak and sauté for 3 minutes until the onion is soft and the meat is browned.
4. Add the beef stock.
5. Press the "meat/stew" button and "adjust" the time to 40 minutes.
6. Once the pot beeps, allow the pot to depressurize and cool down on its own.
7. Remove the lid and give the stew a stir.
8. Serve while hot.
9. ENJOY!

Ham hock soup

This soup is warming, nutritious, tasty, and SO easy to make! Ask your butcher for a ham hock and get that Instant Pot ready!

Serves: 6-8

Ingredients:

- 1 ham hock
- 2 litres water
- 2 celery stalks, roughly chopped
- 2 carrots, roughly chopped
- 1 onion, roughly chopped

Method:

1. Place the ham hock into the Instant Pot, sprinkle with salt and pepper, and cover with water.
2. Press the "meat/stew" button and "adjust" the time to 40 minutes.
3. Once the pot beeps, carefully release the steam, and remove the lid.
4. Take the ham hock out of the pot and keep the water in the pot.
5. With a fork, remove the meat from the ham hock and place it back into the pot with the ham water (it's now a delicious broth).
6. Add the celery, carrot, and onion to the pot and secure the lid.
7. Press the "soup" button and "adjust" the time to 30 minutes.
8. Once the pot beeps, allow the pot to depressurize and cool down on its own.
9. Remove the lid and stir the soup.
10. Serve while hot.
11. ENJOY!

Carrot and capsicum starter soup

This is a "starter" soup because of the carrots. Although carrots are allowed on Keto, they should be limited. I like to have a small cup of this as a light starter or snack when I have some of my carb quota left for the day. Add some chilli to give it a hint of heat!

Serves: about 10 small servings

Ingredients:

- 5 carrots, roughly chopped
- 4 red capsicums, roughly chopped
- 1 onion, roughly chopped
- 2 garlic cloves, finely chopped
- 500ml litre vegetable or chicken stock
- 150ml full-fat cream

Method:

1. Place all ingredients except cream into the Instant Pot and secure the lid onto the pot.
2. Press the "soup" button and "adjust" the time to 25 minutes.
3. Allow the pot to depressurize and cool down on its own.
4. Blend the soup with a stick blender until smooth.
5. Stir the cream through the soup.
6. Serve in small bowls or cups.
7. ENJOY!

Spinach, herb, and sausage soup

You can substitute the spinach for kale or Swiss chard if you prefer, but I love spinach. Salty, savoury sausage is a great soup ingredient, and I'm sure this will become one of your Keto favourites!

Serves: 6

Ingredients:

- 1lb low-carb pork sausages, cut into pieces (don't worry if the meat comes out of the casing a bit, it doesn't matter)
- 1 onion, roughly chopped
- 2 garlic cloves, finely chopped
- 2tbsp olive oil
- 1 carrot, roughly chopped
- 4 cups baby spinach leaves
- 3tsp mixed dried herbs, (thyme, oregano, and rosemary are my favourites)
- 1 litre chicken or vegetable stock
- 1 cup full-fat cream

Method:

1. Press the "sauté" button on your Instant Pot and keep the temperature at "normal".
2. Drizzle the olive oil into the pot.
3. Once the oil is hot, add the garlic, onion, carrot, spinach, sausage, and herbs.
4. Sauté until sizzling and the onion is clear.
5. Add the stock.

6. Secure the lid onto the pot, make sure the steam valve is closed.
7. Press the "soup" button and "adjust" the time to 30 minutes.
8. Allow the pot to depressurize on its own.
9. Remove the lid and stir the cream through the soup.
10. ENJOY!

Cabbage soup (ideal for detoxing and getting "back on track")

I know that cabbage soup doesn't sound very inspiring, but I promise, it's delicious! This is what I eat when I feel like I need to have a bit of a detox, and if I've come close to falling off the Keto road! It's a great light lunch or supper.

Serves: approximately 6

Ingredients:

- 1 head of cabbage (not red cabbage), roughly chopped
- 1 onion, roughly chopped
- 3 garlic cloves, finely chopped
- 1tsp chilli powder
- 30gm butter
- 1 litre chicken stock

Method:

1. Add all ingredients to the Instant Pot and secure the lid onto the pot, make sure the steam valve is closed.
2. Press the "soup" button and "adjust" the time to 25 minutes.
3. Allow the pot to depressurize and cool down on its own.
4. Remove the lid and stir the pot.
5. Serve while hot.
6. ENJOY!

Broccoli soup

For me, broccoli is a major staple of my Keto diet, and soup is an awesome way of getting my broccoli fix. This soup is so creamy and filling, even the most broccoli-averse eaters will love it. You can even fill freezer-proof containers with single soup servings to have on hand when life gets tough and there's no time to cook. A note on onions: large amounts of onions aren't advisable on Keto because of their sugar content, however, one small onion divided between a whole soup is just fine.

Serves: approximately 5 medium servings of soup

Ingredients:

- One large head of broccoli, chopped into small chunks (including the stalks, they're full of good things!)
- 1 small white onion
- Olive oil or butter to sauté (about a tablespoon)
- 1 litre chicken or vegetable stock (homemade is best, but no judgements if it's bought!)
- 200mls heavy cream

Method:

1. Place the onion and butter or oil in the Instant Pot and press the "sauté" button.
2. Stir the onions as they cook and turn transparent.
3. Place the broccoli and the stock into the Instant Pot, place the lid on, and make sure the steam vent is closed.
4. Press the "soup" button on the Instant Pot and "adjust" the time for 30 minutes.

5. Walk away, take a nap...do whatever you like while your soup cooks and depressurizes all on its own.
6. Remove the lid.
7. Use a stick blender (or pour the contents into an upright blender) and process until smooth.
8. Stir the cream through the soup.
9. Serve with a swirl of cream on top and a sprinkling of salt and fresh pepper.
10. ENJOY!

Chicken broth soup

There's something so wholesome and old-timey about chicken broth soup. It reminds me of those romantic movies where the guy brings the girl hot chicken soup when she's sick...wait, why hasn't my partner ever done that for me?! Okay, back to the recipe! In all seriousness, this really is a great soup for when you are feeling under the weather, as it provides the salts and minerals you need, without being too heavy or filling. You can use any pieces of chicken on the bone you like, but I prefer a mixture of thigh and drumsticks.

Serves: approximately 5 medium servings

Ingredients:

- Chicken pieces on the bone – approximately 8 pieces (about 2-3lbs)
- 1 white onion, roughly chopped
- 1tsp olive oil
- 2 long celery stalks, chopped into 3 inch pieces
- 2 large zucchinis (or 3 small) chopped into 2 inch pieces
- 1 dried bay leaf
- Any other fresh herbs you have – thyme, rosemary and oregano are great! A small bunch each
- 4 cups water (or enough to cover the ingredients)

Method:

1. Drizzle the olive oil into the bottom of your Instant Pot and add the onion pieces, zucchini pieces, celery pieces, and herbs into the pot.

2. Place the chicken pieces on top of the vegetables in an even layer if you can.
3. Pour over the water.
4. Place the Instant Pot lid on to the pot, make sure the steam vent is closed.
5. Press the "Soup" button.
6. "Adjust" the time for 25 minutes.
7. Leave the Instant Pot to cook and then depressurize on its own.
8. Once the pot beeps, remove the lid after carefully depressurizing.
9. Remove the chicken pieces and remove the meat with a fork.
10. Take a slotted spoon and remove the herbs and vegetables, discard them.
11. Return the shredded chicken to the soup.
12. ENJOY!

Creamy cauliflower soup

If you're a lover of classics like Leek and Potato soup, then this cauliflower soup will hit the spot! Cauliflower is a delicious vegetable which has risen in popularity over recent years, because it can be used in so many ways (you'll see it again in the recipe section!). Make a big batch of this soup on a cold night, and enjoy the hot, creamy, low-carb nutrition.

Serves: approximately 4

Ingredients:

- 1 head of cauliflower, cut into chunks
- 1 small onion, roughly chopped
- 1 clove of garlic, finely chopped
- 1tbsp olive oil
- 500ml vegetable stock (or enough to just cover the cauliflower)
- 200ml heavy cream

Method:

1. Press the "sauté" button and keep the temperature at "normal".
2. Add the olive oil until heated.
3. Add the onion and garlic and cook until soft (careful not to burn the garlic, keep stirring).
4. Add the cauliflower and stir into the oil, garlic, and onion mixture.
5. Pour the vegetable stock into the pot until it just covers the vegetables.
6. Secure the lid onto the Instant Pot.

7. Change the setting to "soup" and keep the temperature at "normal".
8. "Adjust" the time to 20 minutes and leave it to cook.
9. Once the timer beeps and the pot depressurizes, remove the lid.
10. Puree the soup with a hand-held stick blender.
11. Stir the cream into the soup.
12. Serve in bowls.
13. ENJOY!

Coconut curry soup

This is a spicy soup for those of you who love a kick of heat, and a creamy hit of coconutty-goodness! It's kind of like a laksa, but without the carb-loaded noodles, and complicated ingredient list. Choose a high-quality red curry paste from your local Asian food store, or from the International section at your supermarket. Check the ingredients and make sure they are whole foods with minimal additives. Most curry pastes are low-carb, but double check! We are only using a small amount, so a tiny bit of carbs spread between 4 servings is well below the carb requirements for your daily Keto menu.

Serves: approximately 4

Ingredients:

- 2 cans full-fat coconut milk (approximately 800ml but if your cans are more or less, it's fine)
- 500ml chicken stock
- 2 cloves garlic, finely chopped
- 1 small onion, finely chopped
- 1tbsp olive oil
- 1tbsp red curry paste
- 2 handfuls of baby spinach
- 2 heads of Pak Choi or Bok Choi, steamed (microwave is fine!)

Method:

1. Press the "sauté" button and add the olive oil to the pot
2. Add the garlic and onion, sauté until soft

3. Add the curry paste and stir into the oil until you smell the curry aroma (about 1 minute)
4. Add the coconut milk and stock
5. Secure the lid onto the Instant Pot
6. Press the "soup" button and "adjust" the time to 15 minutes
7. Leave the Instant Pot to do its thing
8. Once the pot beeps and then depressurizes on its own, remove the lid
9. Add the spinach leaves and stir through until the heat wilts them
10. Place the soup into bowls with steamed Asian greens on the side
11. ENJOY!

Slow cooked pork shoulder with buttered green beans

This recipe makes great use of the "slow cook" function on your Instant Pot. Slow cooked pork shoulder is soft, tender, and delicious. Serving the delicious meat with buttery green beans adds a dose of nutrients and freshness. This recipe takes about 4 hours to cook, but you don't need to attend to it as the Instant Pot takes care of it for you. Instant Pot tip: when using the "Slow Cook" setting, it's very important to remember to set the steam release handle to either side of the vent. Make sure the handle is to the left, or to the right, not in the middle as it must leave the vent open.

Serves: approximately 5-6 servings

Ingredients:

- 4lb boneless pork shoulder (ask your butcher to remove the bones if needed) cut into large pieces (each piece about the size of your palm)
- 1tsp paprika
- 1tsp chilli powder
- ½ tsp cinnamon
- 1tsp salt (leave this out if you're using garlic and onion salt instead of fresh garlic and onion)
- 2 cloves garlic, finely chopped (use garlic salt if you prefer, 1tsp)
- 1 small onion, finely chopped (use onion salt if you prefer, 1tsp)
- ¼ cup apple cider vinegar
- 2 cups water
- 2 cups frozen green beans
- 20 grams butter, broken up into small knobs

Method:

1. Add the paprika, chilli powder, cinnamon, salt, onion, garlic (or onion and garlic salts) into a bowl.
2. Add the pork shoulder pieces and rub the dry mix all over the pieces and rub it into the flesh.
3. Press the "slow cook" button on your Instant Pot. Keep the time at the pre-set 4 hours, and the temperature at "normal", no need to adjust these.
4. Place the pork into the pot.
5. Pour over the apple cider vinegar and the water onto the pork.
6. Secure the lid on the Instant Pot and make sure the steam valve is open.
7. Walk away and leave the Instant Pot to slow cook your pork to perfection.
8. 10 minutes before the pork is done, cook the green beans in the microwave for approximately 2 minutes in a covered bowl.
9. Place the knobs on top of the beans so it melts from the heat, sprinkle with salt.
10. Remove the pork pieces from the pot and place onto a chopping board.
11. Use 2 forks to pull the pork flesh apart.
12. Serve pork with buttered green beans.
13. ENJOY!

Spicy lamb stew

Lamb is such a sweet and earthy meat, packed with minerals such as iron. This spicy lamb stew is full of flavour and heat, you will absolutely love it. It freezes well in airtight containers, so keep any leftovers in the freezer for another day. Serve with any greens you wish, but I prefer buttered broccoli!

Serves: approximately 5-6 servings

Ingredients:

- 4pounds lamb (as your butcher for a suitable cut for stews, it's more affordable!), cubed
- 1 onion, diced
- 3 garlic cloves, finely chopped
- 2tbsp olive oil
- Knob of butter (approximately 20 grams but no need to be too precise)
- 2 cans diced tomatoes
- 1tsp chilli powder
- 1tsp paprika
- 1tsp cumin
- 2 cups beef stock

Method:

1. Press the "sauté" button and "adjust" the temperature to "more", so the heat is high.
2. Add a drizzle of olive oil to the pot and heat for about 20 seconds.
3. Add the cubed lamb and sauté until browned but not cooked through, about 5 minutes.

4. Add ALL remaining ingredients, (yup, it's that easy!).
5. Secure the lid onto the Instant Pot.
6. Make sure the steam release handle is on either side of the vent.
7. Press "slow cook".
8. Keep the time at the default 4 hours and keep the temperature at "normal".
9. Walk away and let the Instant Pot slowly cook your lamb.
10. Let the pot depressurize on its own.
11. Remove the lid.
12. Dish the spicy lamb stew into bowls while hot.
13. Serve with a side of green vegetables.
14. ENJOY!

Meat

Meat is a real staple of the Keto diet, (for those who aren't vegetarian or vegan). Red meat offers essential minerals such as iron, so it's a great addition to your weekly menu. These recipes offer a simple approach to cooking meat, and of course, the Instant Pot makes it even simpler! Chicken, beef, lamb, and pork all feature in this section of the recipes, so there's something for everyone.

Instant Pot whole chicken

Cooking a whole chicken is very handy for when you want a quick dinner. Throw some veggies together, and you're done! For this one, you'll need to use the trivet which comes with your Instant Pot. Keep the carcass and use it to make chicken broth!

Serves: makes one whole chicken

Ingredients:

- 1 whole chicken, small enough to fit in the Instant Pot
- 2tbsp olive oil
- Salt and pepper
- 2tsp mixed fresh or dried herbs such as oregano, thyme, and tarragon
- Water

Method:

1. Press the "sauté" button on your Instant pot and "adjust" the temperature to "more".
2. Add the olive oil to the pot.
3. Once the oil is hot, place the chicken into the pot breast-side down.
4. Brown the chicken for a few minutes to brown the skin.
5. Take the chicken out and place the trivet into the pot.
6. Place the chicken onto the trivet, breast-side up.
7. Sprinkle the chicken with salt, pepper, and herbs.
8. Pour about ¾ cup of water into the pot (into the bottom, not onto the chicken!).
9. Secure the lid onto the Instant Pot and make sure the steam valve is closed.
10. Press the "poultry" button and "adjust" the pressure to "high".
11. "Adjust" the time for 30 minutes.
12. Allow the pot to depressurize on its own.
13. Remove the lid, then take out the chicken.
14. ENJOY!

Green chicken curry

Green chicken curry is one of my favourite dishes. It reminds me of Winters when I was a kid. And luckily, it's Keto friendly! (if you leave out the piles of fluffy rice, that is). I use chicken thighs, which are cheaper than chicken breasts, and a lot tastier if you ask me. Choose a good-quality, low-carb green curry paste.

Serves: 6

Ingredients:

- 8 chicken thighs, boneless
- 2tbsp olive oil or coconut oil
- 3tbsp green curry paste
- 2 garlic cloves, finely chopped
- 2 cans full-fat coconut milk (about 800ml)
- 2 cups frozen green beans
- Handful of fresh coriander, chopped, to serve

Method:

1. Press the "sauté" button on your Instant Pot and keep the temperature at "normal".
2. Pour your chosen oil into the pot.
3. Once the oil is hot, add the garlic and curry paste, heat until fragrant, about 2 minutes.
4. Add the chicken to the pot and coat in the curry paste, sauté for about 3 minutes.
5. Pour the coconut milk into the pot.
6. Press "meat/stew" and "adjust" the time to 25 minutes.

7. Secure the lid onto the pot and make sure the steam valve is closed.
8. Once the pot beeps, carefully depressurize the pot manually and remove the lid.
9. Stir the green beans into the hot curry so they defrost and become cooked yet still crunchy.
10. Serve your curry with a sprinkling of fresh coriander.
11. ENJOY!

Corned beef

Corned beef is a very tasty way of getting your red meat intake. It's as delicious cold as it is hot, so you can have a quick and handy lunch waiting in the fridge.

Serves: makes one large corned beef (8-12 servings depending on size)

Ingredients:

- 3lb corned beef silverside
- 5 garlic cloves
- 1tsp pepper corns
- 3 dried bay leaves
- Salt
- 3tbsp apple cider vinegar
- 4 cups water

Method:

1. Place your trivet into the Instant Pot and place the beef on top.
2. Sprinkle the pepper corns, bay leaves, salt, and garlic cloves onto the pot.
3. Pour the vinegar and water into the pot so the beef is covered.
4. Secure the lid onto the pot and make sure the steam valve is closed.
5. Press the "meat/stew" button and "adjust" the time for 90 minutes .
6. Once the pot beeps, either manually release the pressure, or leave it to depressurize naturally.
7. Remove the beef from the liquid, (discard liquid and herbs) and allow it to rest before cutting.
8. ENJOY!

Sticky chicken drumsticks

Chicken drumsticks are so easy to prepare. Serve them with a heaping pile of fresh, steamed greens, and you've got a perfect Keto dinner! This recipe uses lemon juice, garlic, and a dash of soy sauce.

Serves: 4 (2 drumsticks per serving)

Ingredients:

- 8 chicken drumsticks
- Juice of 1 lemon
- 3tbsp olive oil
- 3 garlic cloves, finely chopped
- 1tsp grated fresh ginger (a small amount of fresh ginger is okay on Keto)
- 2tbsp soy sauce

Method:

1. Combine lemon juice, olive oil, garlic, ginger, and soy sauce in your Instant Pot.
2. Add the chicken drumsticks and stir them around to coat them in the sauce.
3. Secure the lid onto the pot and press "poultry".
4. "Adjust" the time for 20 minutes.
5. Allow the pot to depressurize and cool down on its own.
6. Open the pot, take out your drumsticks, spoon out any remaining sauce and pour it over the drumsticks.
7. ENJOY!

Chinese spice pork chops

The combination of sweet pork and Chinese spice is a divine combination, and the Instant Pot cooks this dish in a flash. Make sure to find free-range, ethical pork chops. I like to serve this with buttery beans and broccoli.

Serves: 6

Ingredients:

- 6 pork chops
- 3tbsp olive oil
- 1tbsp apple cider vinegar
- 2tsp Chinese five spice
- Salt and pepper
- Water

Method:

1. Combine the olive oil, apple cider vinegar, Chinese five spice, water, salt, and pepper in a large bowl.
2. Add the pork chops to the bowl and coat them in the marinade, leave for an hour.
3. Press the "sauté" button on your Instant Pot and "adjust" the temperature to "more".
4. Add the pork chops and all of the marinade to the Instant Pot and sauté them for about 2 minutes on both sides to seal.
5. Press the "meat/stew" button and "adjust" the time to 5 minutes.
6. Once the pot beeps, carefully release the pressure manually.
7. Remove the lid.
8. Serve the pork chops with the sauce from the pot.
9. ENJOY!

Beef stroganoff

This Russian classic combines strips of beef, a hint of mustard, and the creamy tang of sour cream. It's usually served with buttered noodles...but on Keto, I find it's just as delicious on its own!

Serves: 6

Ingredients:

- 2lb blade steak, cut into strips
- 1 onion, finely chopped
- 2 garlic cloves, finely chopped
- 2tbsp olive oil
- 1tbsp Dijon mustard
- 2 cups beef stock
- Salt and pepper
- 1 cup full-fat sour cream
- Fresh parsley, finely chopped, to serve

Method:

1. Press the "sauté" button on your Instant Pot and keep the temperature at "normal".
2. Add the olive oil.
3. Once the oil is hot, add the garlic and onion and sauté until soft.
4. Add the mustard and stir into the onion and garlic.
5. Add the beef strips and sauté them in the mustard, onion and garlic for 1 minute.
6. Pour the stock into the pot and add a sprinkle of salt and pepper.

7. Press the "meat/stew" button and "adjust" the time to 20 minutes.
8. Secure the lid onto the pot and make sure the steam valve is closed.
9. Once the pot beeps, allow the pot to depressurize on its own.
10. Open the pot, stir the sour cream through the stroganoff.
11. Serve while hot, with a sprinkle of parsley.
12. ENJOY!

Slow cooked beef with red wine and rosemary

There's something so fancy and elegant about the mixture of beef, lamb, and rosemary. But, as fancy as it tastes, it's SO easy to throw together! Ask your butcher for a cut of chuck steak. Serve with a side of greens, or creamy cauliflower mash (recipe in the "sides" section).

Serves: approximately 6 servings

Ingredients:

- 4lb chuck steak, cut into cubes
- 1 onion, diced
- 3 garlic cloves
- 2tbsp olive oil
- 500ml pinot noir (or any other dry red wine)
- 500ml beef stock
- 1 large sprig of fresh rosemary, (or 2tsp dried if you don't have fresh)

Method:

1. Press the "sauté" button on your instant pot and keep the temperature at "normal".
2. Add the olive oil and heat for 10 seconds.
3. Add the onion and garlic, sauté until soft.
4. Add the beef and sauté for 5 minutes until browned but not cooked.
5. Add the wine, stock, and rosemary.
6. Secure the lid on the Instant Pot and make sure the steam vent is closed.

7. Press the "meat/stew" button and adjust the time to 40 minutes

8. Once the Instant Pot finishes cooking, allow the pot to depressurize on its own.

9. Open the lid and dish out your delicious beef with red wine!

10. ENJOY!

Creamy chicken and mushroom "bake"

Chicken thighs mingle with brown mushrooms, ivory cream, a dash of white wine...heavenly! This is such an easy dish (as most Instant Pot dishes are!) but it's sophisticated enough to serve for a dinner party or date. I would serve this with a side of greens, (see the "sides" section for some ideas). Even though it's called a "bake", it's actually cooked in the Instant Pot with the poultry function.

Serves: 5-6

Ingredients:

- 6 chicken thighs
- 1 onion, finely chopped
- 2 garlic cloves, finely chopped
- 1tbsp olive oil
- 2 cups chopped brown mushrooms
- A couple of sprigs of fresh thyme (1tsp dried if you don't have fresh)
- 100ml dry white wine
- 250ml heavy cream
- 250ml chicken stock

Method:

1. Press the "sauté" button on your Instant Pot and keep the temperature at "normal".
2. Add the olive oil and heat for 10 seconds.
3. Add the onion and garlic, sauté until soft.
4. Add the chicken and sauté on each side until browned but not cooked.

5. Add the mushrooms, stir through until coated in oil and juices, sauté for 2 minutes.
6. Add the wine, cream, chicken stock, and thyme.
7. Secure the lid onto the Instant Pot and make sure the vent is closed.
8. Change the setting by pressing "Poultry".
9. Change the time to 30 minutes.
10. Once the Instant Pot has finished cooking, leave it to release the steam on its own.
11. Remove the lid, dish out and...
12. ENJOY!

Rare beef strips with charred green peppers and yogurt coriander dressing

Rare beef, cut into thin, tender strips is one of my favourite ways of eating red meat. This recipe pairs beef with charred green peppers which gives a delicious, smoky flavour. The yogurt coriander dressing adds a kick of freshness and tang. Any cut of steak is fine, but rib eye is my choice. I like my steak to be really rare, but if you prefer a more well-done steak, then cook it according to your liking! Go ahead and try it!

Serves: 4

Ingredients:

- 4 small steaks (1 small steak per person, or 2 large steaks split between 4)
- 3 green peppers (capsicum), cut into strips
- 1tbsp olive oil
- 1tsp chilli flakes
- ½ cup full-fat, unsweetened Greek yogurt
- Large bunch of coriander (AKA cilantro) finely chopped

Method:

1. Press the "sauté" button on your Instant Pot and "adjust" the temperature to "more".
2. While the pot is heating up, rub the steaks with olive oil and a small sprinkling of cracked black pepper.
3. Once the Instant Pot is hot, place the steaks into the pot and cook for 2 minutes each side, or until you reach your desired of doneness.

4. Remove the steaks from the pot and leave on a board to rest, keep the pot on and don't adjust the temperature.
5. While the meat is resting, drizzle some olive oil into the pot with the steak juices left over from the meat.
6. Add the sliced green peppers and the chilli flakes to the pot and stir as they sauté.
7. Cook the peppers until they are slightly charred and soft.
8. Turn off the Instant Pot.
9. Slice the beef into thin strips and distribute onto serving plates with a serving of peppers.
10. Mix together the coriander and yogurt and add a dollop to each plate.
11. ENJOY!

Lamb and coconut curry with cauliflower rice

This is a real favourite in my house. The sweet lamb, warming spices, creamy coconut, and fluffy cauliflower rice is so comforting and filling. I use diced lamb shoulder for this recipe, but any cut of lamb you find works just as well. The spices used are standard spices you probably have lurking in your cupboard. If you don't have them, they're a great thing to have on hand as they add such great flavour and depth to your dishes. While spices do have carbs in them, we only add a very small amount to our dishes, so there's no need to worry about ruining ketosis.

Serves: approximately 6

Ingredients:

- 2lb lamb, cut into cubes
- 2tbsp olive oil
- 1 onion, finely chopped
- 2 garlic cloves, finely chopped
- 1/2tsp ground turmeric
- 1tsp ground cumin
- 1/2tsp ground coriander
- 1tsp chilli powder
- 400ml full-fat coconut milk
- 500ml beef stock
- 1 tin chopped tomatoes
- 1 head of cauliflower, cut into rough chunks
- Knob of butter (about 1tbsp)

Method:

1. Press the "sauté" button on your Instant Pot and "adjust" the temperature to "more".
2. Add a drizzle of olive oil to the pot and heat for 10 seconds.
3. Add the lamb cubes to the pot and brown them for about 3 minutes.
4. Add the onion, garlic, and spices to the pot and coat the lamb in them by stirring it all together.
5. Add the stock, tinned tomatoes, and coconut milk to the pot.
6. Secure the lid onto the pot and change the setting by pressing the "meat/stew" button, make sure the steam valve is closed.
7. "adjust" the timer to 20 minutes.
8. Allow the Instant Pot to depressurize and cool down on its own.
9. Meanwhile, add the cauliflower to a blender and blitz until it resembles the size and consistency of rice.
10. Tip the cauliflower into a microwave-proof bowl, place the knob of butter on top of the cauliflower, cover, then place into the microwave.
11. Cook cauliflower in the microwave on High for about 3 minutes.
12. Stir through the melted butter and add a sprinkle of salt and pepper.
13. Serve the lamb curry on a bed of cauliflower rice.
14. ENJOY!

Keto Carbonara with bacon and cream

You might be wondering why this one is in the "meat" section, as the only meaty ingredient is bacon...but I just had to include it! It's so delicious and luxurious, without ruining Ketosis. If you don't have a spiralizer to make your Keto zucchini pasta, you can just use a vegetable peeler to peel thin slices of zucchini for a fettucine-style pasta alternative.

Serves: 4

Ingredients:

- 5 large zucchinis, "spiralized" or peeled thinly to resemble fettucine or spaghetti
- 4 rashers of streaky bacon, chopped into 1cm pieces
- 1 garlic clove, finely chopped
- 200ml heavy cream
- ¼ cup grated parmesan cheese

Method:

1. Press the "sauté" button on your Instant Pot and "adjust" the temperature to "more".
2. Add the olive oil, garlic, and bacon pieces to the pot and sauté until the bacon is sizzling and the garlic has softened.
3. Add the zucchini pasta and coat with the oil and bacon.
4. Sauté the zucchini pasta until slightly soft.
5. Add the cream and parmesan cheese and stir through.
6. Cook for about 5 minutes on the "sauté" function, stirring to make sure it doesn't catch on the bottom of the pot, until the cream is thickened and the zucchini is soft.
7. Turn off the Instant Pot.
8. Serve the carbonara into bowls while hot!
9. ENJOY!

Ground beef chili with yogurt and avocado topping

As we know, there are no beans allowed on the Keto diet, but we can still enjoy chili! This recipe is simple and easy, but it mimics the warming feel of a hot chili, without the carbs. Ground meat is affordable and incredibly versatile, (as you'll see below!). I love adding yogurt and avocado on top of this chili, it gives a real "nacho night" vibe, with a good hit of healthy fats.

Serves: approximately 6

Ingredients:

- 2lb ground beef
- 1 onion, finely chopped
- 1 garlic clove, finely chopped
- 1tbsp olive oil
- 2 cans tinned chopped tomatoes
- 1tsp paprika
- 1tsp chilli power
- 1tsp cumin
- 1tsp cinnamon
- 1tbsp full-fat Greek yogurt per serving
- 2 avocadoes, scooped out and mashed (or sliced/cubed, go with your preference!)

Method:

1. Press the "sauté" button on your Instant Pot and keep the temperature at "normal".
2. Drizzle the olive oil into the pot and heat for 10 seconds.
3. Add the onion and garlic and heat until soft.

4. Add the ground beef, stir it into the oil and brown it for about 3 minutes.
5. Add the spices and tinned tomatoes to the pot and stir to combine.
6. Secure the lid onto the Instant Pot and make sure the steam vent is closed.
7. Press the "bean/chili" button and "adjust" the time to 15 minutes.
8. Allow the Instant Pot to depressurize on its own and remove the lid when it's done.
9. Serve the chili with a dollop of full-fat Greek yogurt and some fresh avocado on top.
10. ENJOY!

Cheesy meatballs with tomato sauce

I don't know about you, but I LOVE meatballs, especially when they're loaded with oozy, melted cheese. This recipe uses pork mince, but you can use ANY meat you like. These meatballs bathe in a deliciously rich tomato sauce with a slight hint of heat from flaked chilli. I like to make a batch of these meatballs and tomato sauce on a Sunday and pack servings of it away for lunch during the week. The "sauté" function and the "meat/stew" function is used in this recipe. The "sauté" function browns the meatballs, and the "meat/stew" function cooks the meatballs in the tomato sauce for only 5 minutes! So quick, so easy.

Serves: approximately 5 (4 meatballs per serving)

Ingredients:

- 2.5lb minced meat
- 1 cup grated cheese (I like to use mozzarella, but you can use any cheese)
- 2 garlic cloves, finely chopped
- 1 onion, finely chopped
- 1tbsp olive oil
- 1tsp chopped fresh parsley
- 1 litre tomato passata (or 3 cans of tinned chopped tomatoes)
- 1tsp chilli flakes
- 1tsp apple cider vinegar

Method:

1. In a large bowl, mix together the ground meat, garlic, onion, cheese, and parsley.
2. Roll the meat mixture into 20 even-sized balls and place on a plate or board.
3. Press the "sauté" button on your Instant Pot and keep the temperature at "normal".
4. Add the olive oil to the pot and heat for 10 seconds.
5. Once the oil is hot, add the meatballs in groups of about 7 and cook for about 3 minutes until browned.
6. Once all of the meatballs are browned, return them all to the Instant Pot.
7. Pour the passata or tinned tomatoes into the pot.
8. Add the chilli flakes and apple cider vinegar to the pot.
9. Secure the lid onto the Instant Pot and make sure the steam valve is closed.
10. Change the setting by pressing the "meat/stew" button.
11. "Adjust" the time for 5 minutes.
12. Let the Instant Pot depressurize on its own before removing the lid.
13. Serve with greens...or on its own!
14. ENJOY!

Ground lamb burgers

Don't tell me you don't like burgers, EVERYONE likes burgers! And just because these ones are low-carb, it doesn't mean they aren't as good as "regular" burgers. The juicy lamb patties with melted cheese and fresh tomatoes are so delicious, you'll never want a Big Mac again. The "bun" comes in the form of fresh, crunchy iceberg lettuce. I love this recipe for Friday or Saturday nights when I want something a little more fun and reminiscent of a takeaway dinner. The fresh mint and parsley gives a garden-fresh hint of flavour. Don't be freaked out by the "steam" function used in this recipe. Steaming patties to melt the cheese and keep the meat juicy is an old burger technique, and it works!

Serves: makes 6 burger patties

Ingredients:

For the patties
- 2lb ground lamb
- 1 garlic clove, finely chopped
- ½ onion, finely chopped
- 1 egg, lightly beaten
- 2tsp freshly parsley, finely chopped
- 1tsp fresh mint, finely chopped
- Salt and pepper to season
- 2tbsp olive oil

For assembling the burgers:
- 2 leaves of iceberg lettuce per burger
- 2 slices of fresh tomato per burger
- 1 large slice of cheese per burger (I use cheddar)
- 1tsp low-carb mustard per burger

Method:

1. In a large bowl, mix together the ground lamb, garlic, onion, egg, salt, pepper, parsley, and mint.
2. Shape the meat mixture into 6 patties (as thick or thin as you like!)
3. Press the "Sauté" button on your Instant Pot and keep the temperature at "normal".
4. Drizzle some olive oil into the pot and heat for 10 seconds.
5. Add the patties, 3 at a time, and cook for 2 minutes each side, or until golden brown.
6. Once all of the patties are cooked and brown, place them in a single layer on a rack or basket inside your Instant Pot.
7. Pour ¼ cup of water into the bottom of the Instant Pot.
8. Secure the lid and close the steam valve.
9. Change the setting by pressing "steam".
10. Change the time to "3" minutes.
11. Wait for the Instant Pot to finish steaming and release the valve.
12. Once the steam as fully escaped, open the Instant Pot and take out the patties.
13. Assemble the patties onto the lettuce "buns" with your desired low-carb toppings.
14. ENJOY!

Beef steaks with creamy blue cheese sauce

If you're not a fan of blue cheese, then this recipe is certainly not for you. You could replace the blue cheese sauce with creamy mushrooms or spinach (see the "sides" section). Because blue cheese can be a little more expensive than other ingredients, this is more of a "special occasion" dish, for a birthday, anniversary, or date. This recipe contains butter, cream, and blue cheese, so it's devilishly rich and creamy! My choice of meat is eye fillet.

Serves: 4

Ingredients:

- 4 steaks, size and cut of your choice
- Olive oil to rub into steaks
- 1 garlic clove, cut in half lengthways
- 1tsp butter per steak

For the sauce:
- 100gm blue cheese
- 1tbsp butter
- 1 garlic clove, finely chopped
- 200ml heavy cream
- 100ml dry white wine

Method:

1. If the steaks are in the fridge, take them out and leave them to reach room temperature.
2. Rub the room temperature steaks with the cut garlic to infuse the flavour into the meat.

3. Rub the steaks with olive oil to moisten, and add a pinch of cracked pepper if you like.
4. Make the sauce while the steaks sit and the garlic infuses into them.
5. Press the "sauté" button on your Instant Pot and keep the temperature at "normal".
6. Had the butter to the pan and heat until melted.
7. Add the garlic to the melted butter in the pan and heat for about 1 minute.
8. Add the white wine and "cook off" the alcohol for about 1 minute.
9. Add the blue cheese and cream, stir while the cheese melts.
10. Once the cheese has melted, leave the sauce to thicken for about 1 minute, you still want it to be a pourable consistency.
11. You can either grill the steaks on a BBQ or griddle pan, or cook them in the Instant Pot using the "sauté" function, but you'll just have to clean it out since you've just made the sauce in it.
12. Once the steak is cooked to your liking, leave it to rest for 5 minutes.
13. Pour a generous serving of blue cheese sauce over the steaks right before serving.
14. ENJOY! (I mean really, how could you *not* enjoy this one?!)

Seafood

Fish is an excellent source of Omega 3's and fatty oils which are great for our brain, skin, hair, and waistlines. Here we have a few different options for fish and seafood to suit different tastes and occasions. Some of these recipes are ideal for Keto-friendly dinner parties when you want to serve something tasty and low-carb, such as the "Spicy prawns with fresh mint dip". I recommend buying fresh fish on the day that you intend to eat it.

Seafood chowder

This creamy fish chowder is mouth wateringly good. The bacon gives a lovely saltiness, while the cream ensures a rich and decadent flavour.

Serves: 4-6 (4 large servings, 6 starter-size servings)

Ingredients:

- 1 ½lb white fish, cut into chunks
- 3 rashers of streaky bacon, cut into small pieces
- Olive oil
- 2 garlic cloves, finely chopped
- 1 onion, finely chopped
- Salt and pepper
- 1tsp mixed dried herbs such as thyme, basil, oregano, and marjoram
- 500ml full-fat cream
- 400ml fish stock or chicken stock
- Fresh parsley, finely chopped, to serve

Method:

1. Press "sauté" on your Instant Pot and keep the temperature at "normal".
2. Add the olive oil to the pot.
3. Once the oil is hot, add the onion, garlic, herbs, and bacon, cook until the onion is soft and the bacon is sizzling.
4. Add the stock, salt, and pepper, and fish.
5. Press the "meat/stew" button and "adjust" the time to 5 minutes.
6. Once the pot beeps, carefully release the pressure and remove the lid.
7. Stir the cream through the soup.
8. ENJOY!

Easy fish skewers with veggies

Skewers are a genius way of serving fish and veggies. Not only are they great for dinner parties or large groups, they're ideal for quick dinners for one or two! Use any low-carb, seasonal vegetables you have on hand. This recipe uses green capsicums, eggplant, and zucchini.

Serves: makes 10 skewers (I eat about 3 or 4 per serving)

Ingredients:

- 2 large fillets of white fish of your choice, cut into chunks
- 1 eggplant (aubergine), chopped into chunks the same size as the fish
- 2 green peppers, cut into fifths (seeds and inners removed)
- 2 zucchinis, cut into chunks the same size as the fish
- Olive oil
- Salt and pepper
- 10 wooden skewers (before filling, make sure they fit into your Instant Pot, chop them to size if they're too long)

Method:

1. Load the skewers with equal amounts of fish, eggplant, peppers, and zucchinis by alternating between fish and vegetables until the skewer is filled.
2. Rub each filled skewer with olive oil and sprinkle each skewer with salt and pepper.
3. Pour ½ cup of water into the bottom of the Instant Pot.

4. Press the "steam" button on your Instant Pot and "adjust" the time to 3 minutes.
5. Place the skewers into the basket which came with your Instant Pot (or something similar), if they don't all fit, then you might have to do 2 batches.
6. Secure the lid onto the Instant Pot and make sure the steam valve is closed.
7. Once the pot beeps after 3 minutes, carefully release the steam and remove the lid, take out the skewers.
8. If you need to do another batch of skewers, do it now, adding more water to the pot if the water has evaporated.
9. Once the skewers have all been steamed, tip the water out of the pot.
10. Press the "sauté" button and "adjust" the temperature to "more".
11. Drizzle about a tablespoon of olive oil into the pot.
12. Once the oil is hot, add about 3 skewers at a time to the pot and sauté on each side for about 20 seconds each, or until the fish and vegetables are golden and slightly charred.
13. Serve with any low-carb condiments you like! I like to serve them with Greek yogurt mixed with fresh mint.
14. ENJOY!

Double salmon, cream cheese, and cucumber rolls

These rolls are full of rich salmon flavour. Inside the smoked salmon and cucumber outer, you will bite into a tangy, creamy filling with a piece of delicious steamed salmon. I like to eat these as a special snack, or as a starter before a main meal.

Serves: 4 as a starter or light snack

Ingredients:

- ½ cucumber, very thinly sliced lengthways
- 50gm smoked salmon
- 1 fresh salmon fillet
- Olive oil
- Pepper
- 200gm full-fat cream cheese

Method:

1. Rub the salmon fillet with olive oil and pepper, (I don't add salt because the cream cheese and smoked salmon is already quite salty).
2. Place the salmon fillet in the basket which came with your Instant Pot.
3. Pour ½ cup of water into the bottom of the pot and place the basket with the salmon inside, into the pot.
4. Secure the lid onto the pot and make sure the steam valve is closed.
5. Press "steam" on your instant pot and "adjust" the time for 4 minutes.
6. When the pot beeps, carefully depressurize the pot and open the lid.

7. Take the salmon out of the pot and leave to cool.
8. On a large board, lay out a piece of smoked salmon.
9. Place a strip of cucumber onto the salmon.
10. Evenly dollop or spread the cream cheese onto the smoked salmon.
11. Place a piece of steamed salmon on top of the cream cheese, on the bottom quarter of the strip.
12. Roll up like a sushi roll, so that the salmon is the outer layer, then the cucumber, then the cream cheese and steamed salmon in the middle.
13. You can put a toothpick through the roll to keep it together if you like.
14. ENJOY!

Steamed oysters with red onion and vinegar

Oysters are a luxurious, romantic, and delicious choice for a special occasion. Steaming is my favourite way of cooking oysters, and the red onion and vinegar really ramps up the flavour.

Serves: 2 (multiply the recipe if you're serving more than 2)

Ingredients:

- 10 oysters
- ½ red onion, very finely chopped
- ¼ cup red wine vinegar
- 2tbsp olive oil
- Salt and pepper

Method:

1. Wash the oysters and place them in the basket which came with your Instant Pot.
2. Pour 1 cup of water into the bottom of the pot.
3. Place the basket into the pot.
4. Secure the lid onto the pot and make sure the steam valve is closed.
5. Press the "steam" button on your instant pot and "adjust" the time for 2 minutes.
6. While the oysters steam, mix together the onion, vinegar, olive oil, and salt in a small bowl.
7. Once the pot beeps, carefully depressurize it and open the lid.
8. Take the oysters out of the basket and open the shells.
9. Spoon a teaspoon full of the onion and vinegar mixture over each oyster.
10. ENJOY!

Fish stew

Forgive me for including this recipe in the "seafood" section, and not the "stew" section! Stew is such a great way of enjoying fish. This recipe is incredibly easy, tasty, and of course, low-carb.

Serves: 6

Ingredients:

- 2lb white fish, chopped into chunks
- 1 onion, finely chopped
- 4 garlic cloves, finely chopped
- 4tbsp olive oil
- Salt and pepper
- 1 can tinned chopped tomatoes (about 400gm)
- 200ml dry white wine
- 500ml fish stock
- 1tsp mixed dried herbs such as oregano, thyme, and basil
- Fresh parsley, chopped, to serve

Method:

1. Press the "sauté" button on your Instant Pot and keep the temperature at "normal".
2. Pour the olive oil into the pot.
3. Once the oil is hot, add the garlic and onion, and sauté until the onion is soft.
4. Add the white wine to the pot and reduce for about 1 minute.

5. Add the tomatoes, stock, salt, pepper, herbs and fish to the pot.
6. Press the "meat/stew" button and "adjust" the time to 10 minutes.
7. Allow the pot to depressurize on its own and remove the lid.
8. Serve the stew while hot, with a sprinkling of fresh parsley.
9. ENJOY!

Keto-crumbed fish fingers (great for kids)

Fish fingers are such a reminiscent food for me, as I remember eating them greedily as a child. This is a more sophisticated recipe, using fresh fish and parmesan cheese.

Serves: 4 (3 fingers each)

Ingredients:

- 4 fillets of white fish such as snapper or cod
- 2 eggs, lightly beaten
- salt and pepper
- ½ cup finely grated parmesan
- 3tbsp ground almond
- 3tbsp olive oil
- 1tbsp butter

Method:

1. Mix together the parmesan cheese, ground almonds, salt, and pepper and tip it onto a plate, so the fish can be rolled into it.
2. Slice the fish fillets into 3 pieces (or 4, depending on how large the fillets are).
3. Dip each piece of fish into the beaten egg until lightly coated with egg.
4. After coating each piece of fish in egg, transfer it straight to the plate of crumb mixture and roll it around in the mixture until fully coated.
5. Press the "sauté" button on your Instant Pot and keep the temperature at "normal".

6. Add the olive oil and butter to the pot and heat until the butter is melted.
7. Add the fish pieces to the pot in groups of 4, so that they don't become crowded.
8. Cook for 2-3 minutes each side, or until golden brown.
9. Lay the fish fingers on a plate lined with paper towels as you remove them from the pot.
10. Serve as a snack, starter, finger food, or light dinner with a side salad!
11. ENJOY!

Spicy prawns with fresh mint dip

The combination of spicy chilli and fresh mint makes these prawns so addictively delicious. These are great to serve when you have guests over and you want to impress them without ruining your Ketosis. Because seafood requires such little cooking time, this is a super-fast and easy recipe to rely on whenever you need a tasty dish.

Serves: serves about 6 as a starter

Ingredients:

- 2lb frozen prawns
- 2 garlic cloves, finely chopped
- 1 fresh red chilli, finely chopped
- 2tbsp olive oil

For the mint dip:
- 1 large handful of fresh mint leaves, finely chopped
- 3tbsp olive oil
- 1/4tsp lemon rind
- ½ garlic clove, crushed
- Pinch of salt

Method:

1. Make the dip by combining mint, olive oil, lemon rind, salt, and garlic in a blender and combine until emulsified and at a dipping consistency, add more oil if it's too thick.
2. Set the dip aside while you prepare the prawns.
3. Tip the prawns into a large bowl.

4. Add garlic, chilli, and olive oil and mix the prawns with your hands until they are evenly coated.
5. Tip the prawns into a metal basket and place it in the Instant Pot.
6. Tip ¼ cup water into the bottom of the Instant Pot (careful not to pour it over the prawns!).
7. Press the "steam" button on your Instant Pot and set the timer for 3 minutes.
8. Secure the lid on the pot and make sure the vent is closed.
9. Once the pot beeps, carefully release the steam valve.
10. Remove the lid and tip the prawns onto a serving plate or bowl.
11. Serve with a side of toothpicks so guests (or you!) can pick up the prawns easily.
12. Dip each prawn into the minty dip and...
13. ENJOY!

Fish cakes with lemony cream cheese dip

Fish cakes are a great way of getting your weekly serve of fish, and the lemony creamy cheese dip makes them even more irresistible. This recipe uses white fish, fresh herbs, and only a few other ingredients...easy!

Serves: approximately 6

Ingredients:

- 1 ½ - 2 lbs white fish fillets
- 2 eggs, lightly beaten
- 1tsp fresh parsley, finely chopped
- 1tsp fresh chives, finely chopped
- 1/2tsp chilli powder
- ½ cup coconut flour
- 2tbsp olive oil

For the dip:
- 1 block full-fat cream cheese (about 250gm)
- ½ cup full-fat Greek yogurt
- Finely grated rind of 1 lemon
- Juice of 1 lemon
- Salt and pepper to season

Method:

1. Make the dip first by placing cream cheese, yogurt, lemon rind and juice, salt, and pepper to a bowl and stir to combine. It might take a bit of elbow grease to incorporate the cream cheese into the yogurt as it can be quite firm sometimes.

2. Put the dip aside while you make the fish cakes.
3. Have the coconut flour standing by in a bowl for when you need to coat the cakes.
4. Place the fish fillets into a metal basket in an even layer.
5. Tip ¼ cup water into the Instant Pot and press the "steam" button.
6. "Adjust" the time to 2 minutes.
7. Secure the lid onto the Instant Pot and make sure the vent is closed.
8. Once the pot beeps, open the steam valve so the steam can release.
9. Open the lid and remove the fish.
10. Place the fish into a large bowl and allow it to cool slightly.
11. Add the eggs, parsley, chives, and chilli powder to the bowl.
12. With a fork, mash the fish into the other ingredients until combined.
13. Remove even amounts of fish mixture with a large spoon and shape into patty/cake shapes.
14. Roll each patty into the coconut flour and place onto a plate until all the mixture has been used up.
15. Press the "Sauté" button on the Instant Pot and keep the temperature at "normal".
16. Pour the olive oil into the pot and heat for 10 seconds.
17. Place about 4 fish cakes at a time into the pot and cook each side for about 3 minutes, or until golden.
18. Once all cakes are cooked, turn of the Instant Pot.
19. Serve the fish cakes with the lemony dip in a bowl.
20. ENJOY!

Salmon and coconut "soup"

To me, salmon is the "most glam" of the seafood world. The soft pink colour, the delicate oiliness, and the gorgeous richness makes for a truly satisfying meal. This recipe uses the "soup" function to very quickly poach the salmon in spice-laced coconut milk. If you have a local fish store, treat yourself to some fresh salmon. Otherwise, frozen salmon will work too.

Serves: 4-6

Ingredients:

- 3 large fillets of salmon (½ large fillet per person) cut into large chunks
- 2 cans full-fat coconut milk (about 800ml)
- 250ml fish stock
- 2 garlic cloves, finely chopped
- 1 fresh red chilli, finely chopped (leave out if you or your guests don't like a lot of spice!)
- 1tbsp red curry paste

Method:

1. Press the "sauté" button on your Instant Pot and keep the temperature at "normal".
2. Add the olive oil to the pot and heat for 10 seconds.
3. Add the garlic, chilli, and curry paste, heat for 1 min or until the paste is fragrant.
4. Add the salmon pieces and gently stir into the paste to coat.
5. Pour in the coconut milk and fish stock.
6. Change the setting by pressing "soup".

7. Secure the lid onto the Instant Pot and make sure the steam valve is closed.
8. "Adjust" the time for 6 minutes (salmon does not take long to cook!).
9. Carefully open the steam valve to let the steam escape.
10. Remove the lid.
11. Dish each serving of salmon into a bowl and then ladle over equal amounts of coconut sauce.
12. ENJOY!

Fish burgers with tangy ricotta dressing

ANY kind of burger is a winner in my opinion, but there's something so fresh and wholesome about a fish burger. The tangy ricotta dressing really cuts through the fish and creates a beautiful balance of flavours. Make sure you choose really fresh, crunchy iceberg lettuce for your burger "buns"!

Serves: makes 4 burgers

Ingredients:

- 4 fillets of white fish of your choice
- 2 eggs, lightly beaten
- 2tbsp ground flaxseed
- 3tbsp finely grated parmesan cheese
- 2tbsp ground almonds
- Salt and pepper

For the ricotta dressing:
- ¾ cup full-fat ricotta
- ¼ cup full-fat Greek yogurt
- 1tbsp fresh lemon juice
- ½ garlic clove, crushed

To assemble to burgers:
- 2 large leaves of iceberg lettuce per burger
- Fresh tomato slices
- Any other low carb fresh veggies you like! Cucumber and capsicum are great

Method:

1. Combine the flaxseed, parmesan, almonds, salt, and pepper in a large bowl (this is the "crumb").
2. Coat each fish fillet in the beaten egg.
3. Transfer immediately to the bowl of "crumb" and make sure each fillet is evenly coated.
4. Press the "sauté" button on your Instant Pot and keep the temperature at "normal".
5. Add the olive oil to the pot and heat.
6. Once the olive oil is hot, cook each fillet one at a time, about 3 minutes on each side, or until golden brown.
7. For the ricotta dressing, simply combine ricotta, Greek yogurt, garlic, and lemon juice in a bowl, easy!
8. Assemble the burgers with lettuce, tomato, fish, ricotta dressing, and any other low-carb additions you like.
9. ENJOY!

Fish tacos

These low-carb fish tacos are fully of spice, tang, freshness, and crunch. I like to gently steam the fish in the Instant Pot as it ensures a juicy and tender result. Crispy and fresh iceberg lettuce comes in handy again with this recipe! Instead of carb-loaded taco shells, you can enjoy the crunch of fresh lettuce instead.

Serves: makes 6-8 tacos

Ingredients:

- 4 fillets of white fish of your choice, cut into quarters
- 2tbsp fresh coriander, finely chopped
- 2tbsp fresh lime juice
- 2tsp fresh red chilli, finely chopped
- 2tbsp red onion, finely chopped
- 3tbsp olive oil

To assemble the tacos:
- 1 large iceberg lettuce leaf per taco
- Full-fat sour cream, about 2tsp per taco
- Pickled Jalapenos, (if you like the heat!)

Method:

1. Place the pieces of fish into a large bowl.
2. Add the coriander, lime juice, chilli, red onion, and olive oil and stir until combined and coated.
3. Leave to marinade in the fridge for about an hour.
4. Press the "meat/stew" button and "adjust" the time to 3 minutes.

5. Tip the fish and marinade into the Instant Pot and secure the lid, make sure the steam vent is closed.
6. Once the Instant Pot is finished cooking, release the steam vent immediately to stop the cooking process.
7. Remove the lid and take out the fish.
8. Flake the fish with a fork.
9. Assemble the tacos by placing fish, sour cream, jalapenos, and any other low-carb toppings you like into the lettuce leaves.
10. ENJOY!

Spicy salmon sushi rolls with avocado

Just because you're on Keto, it doesn't mean you have to be deprived of sushi! These Keto sushi rolls are packed with veggies and spicy salmon. You won't even notice that there's no rice! these are great for lunch or a light dinner, (or if you're anything like me...ANY time). There's a small amount of carrot in these sushi rolls, but not enough to ruin Ketosis whatsoever. I like to use the "meat/stew" function on my Instant Pot to cook the salmon, because it makes for a soft and juicy texture if you only cook for a few minutes.

Serves: makes 4 rolls (which makes about 24 pieces if each roll is cut into 6)

Ingredients:

- 1 large fillet of salmon, bones removed, cut into 4 chunks
- 1tbsp olive oil
- 1tsp sesame oil
- 1 red chilli, finely chopped
- Pinch of salt
- A handful of lettuce, I like to use butter lettuce or any other soft variety
- 1 carrot, thinly sliced
- 1 red capsicum, thinly sliced
- Half a cucumber, thinly sliced
- 1 avocado, sliced
- 1tbsp toasted sesame seeds
- 4 nori sheets, (dried seaweed sheets)
- Soy sauce for dipping

Method:

1. Place the salmon pieces in a bowl and rub them with the olive oil, sesame oil, chilli, and a pinch of salt.
2. Press the "meat/stew" button on your Instant Pot and "adjust" the time for 3 minutes.
3. Place the salmon into the pot and secure the lid, making sure the steam valve is closed.
4. Once the timer beeps, immediately open the steam valve (carefully!) so the fish doesn't continue to cook.
5. Open the lid and remove the salmon.
6. To assemble the sushi: lay the nori sheets on a sushi mat if you have one, or else just lay it flat on a board. Place a layer of lettuce onto the bottom quarter of the nori sheet, then place a line of carrots, capsicum, avocado, and cucumber on top of the lettuce. Place a line of salmon on top of the vegetables and sprinkle with toasted sesame seeds.
7. Tightly roll the sushi by bringing it towards you as you roll it up.
8. Seal the edge of the roll once it has been rolled, by rubbing some warm water along the edge of the nori sheet so it is fully closed.
9. Carefully slice the sushi roll into 6 pieces with a sharp knife.
10. Dip into soy sauce (make sure it's low-carb).
11. ENJOY!

Herb encrusted fish with sesame greens

Fresh fish with herbs, greens, and sesame seeds...sounds amazing, right? I opt for this dish all the time as a filling yet light dinner. Choose any fresh, white fish you like.

Serves: 4

Ingredients:

- 4 fillets of fresh fish
- 4tbsp fresh herbs, chopped (any fresh herbs such as parsley, basil, thyme work really well, grab a big mixture from your garden if you can!)
- 2tbsp olive oil
- 1tbsp butter
- 4 bunches of Asian greens such as Bok choy
- 2tbsp sesame seeds, lightly toasted
- Salt and pepper

Method:

1. Coat the fish in a light layer of olive oil and sprinkle them with salt and pepper.
2. Place the chopped herbs on a plate and roll each fillet in the herbs to coat.
3. Place 1 cup of water in the bottom of the Instant Pot.
4. Place the Asian greens into the steaming basket and put the basket into the pot.
5. Press the "steam" button and "adjust" the time to 3 minutes.
6. Secure the lid onto the pot and make sure the steam valve is closed.

7. Once the pot beeps, carefully release the steam and take out the greens.
8. Sprinkle the greens with salt, pepper, and sesame seeds.
9. Press the "sauté" button on your Instant Pot and keep the temperature at "normal".
10. Add the olive oil and butter to the put and heat until the butter is melted.
11. Add the fish fillets to the pot and fry each side for about 3 minutes.
12. Serve the fish with a generous pile of greens.
13. ENJOY!

Vegetarian and Vegan

Vegetables are the best source of vitamins and minerals, so I think vegetarians and vegans have the right idea! Even if you are a meat and dairy eater, you can still enjoy these vegetarian (V) and vegan (V) recipes.

Whole roasted cauliflower with olives and slivered almonds (VG, V)

Cauliflower has become a superstar in the health food world. One of the trendiest ways to cook and serve this creamy-white vegetable is to roast it whole! This recipe uses olives and almonds...the combination is mind blowing.

Serves: makes one whole cauliflower (serves 6-8)

Ingredients:

- 1 whole cauliflower, leaves and outer stalks removed and main stem trimmed
- 3tbsp olive oil
- 10-12 black olives, cut into quarters
- 3tbsp slivered almonds, lightly toasted
- 1tsp paprika
- ½ tsp chilli flakes
- Salt and pepper

Method:

1. Place the cauliflower in the steaming basket which came with your Instant Pot (or something similar).
2. Pour ½ cup of water into the bottom of the pot.
3. Place the basket into the pot and secure the lid onto the pot, make sure the steam valve is closed.
4. Press the "steam" button on your Instant Pot and "adjust" the time for 5 minutes.
5. Once the pot beeps, carefully release the steam and remove the pot.
6. Remove the cauliflower and tip the water out of the pot.
7. Press the "sauté" button on your Instant Pot and keep the temperature at "normal".
8. Rub the cauliflower with olive oil and sprinkle with salt and pepper.
9. Pour a little more olive oil into the pot.
10. Once the oil in the pot is hot, place the cauliflower into the pot, upside down (stalk side up).
11. Sauté the cauliflower for a few minutes, moving it around to ensure the whole top surface becomes golden.
12. Once the cauliflower is cooked, take it out and sprinkle the olives, paprika, almonds, and chilli over the top of it.
13. Cut it into slices and serve.
14. ENJOY!

Goat cheese and pumpkin salad with avocado (V)

Pumpkin and goat cheese go together so well, and the addition of avocado makes this salad even more wonderful. There's only a small amount of pumpkin in this salad, for Keto reasons, but there's plenty of gorgeous spinach, avocado, and goat cheese to savour.

Serves: 4

Ingredients:

- 200gm pumpkin, skin removed, cut into small chunks
- 4 cups baby spinach
- 200gm goat cheese, crumbled into small pieces
- 1 large avocado, flesh cut into small cubes
- 3tbsp olive oil
- 1 garlic clove, finely chopped
- 1tbsp apple cider vinegar
- 3tbsp walnuts, toasted and chopped
- Salt and pepper

Method:

1. Place the pumpkin into the steaming basket which came with your Instant Pot, sprinkle the pumpkin with salt.
2. Pour ½ cup water into the bottom of the Instant Pot.
3. Place the basket of pumpkin into the pot and secure the lid closed, make sure the steam valve is closed.
4. Press the "steam" button and "adjust" the time to 5 minutes.
5. Once the pot beeps, carefully release the steam and remove the lid.

6. Take out the basket of pumpkin and pour the water out of the pot.
7. Press the "sauté" button on the Instant Pot and keep the temperature at "normal".
8. Pour the olive oil into the pot and add the garlic.
9. Once the oil is hot, return the pumpkin to the pot and stir to coat with olive oil and garlic, sauté for 5 minutes or until the pumpkin becomes golden and fried.
10. In a large bowl, combine the spinach leaves, goat cheese, walnuts, avocado, and pumpkin.
11. Combine apple cider vinegar and olive oil in a small cup and pour it over the salad and toss together.
12. ENJOY!

Eggplant poached in coconut milk, with coriander and chilli

Eggplant is an underrated vegetable in my opinion, and this dish really showcases its true deliciousness. Coconut milk, coriander, chilli, and garlic come together to form an amazing dish for vegetarians and vegans.

Serves: 4

Ingredients:

- 2 eggplants, cut into small chunks
- 2tbsp olive oil
- 2 garlic cloves, finely chopped or crushed
- 1 small fresh red chilli, finely chopped (remove some of the seeds if you don't want it to be too spicy)
- ½ tsp ground turmeric
- ½ tsp ground cumin
- Salt and pepper
- 2 cans full-fat coconut milk (about 800ml)
- Large handful fresh coriander, finely chopped

Method:

1. Press the "sauté" button on your Instant Pot and keep the temperature at "normal".
2. Add the olive oil to the pot.
3. Once the oil is hot, add the garlic, chilli, turmeric, and cumin and sauté for about 30 seconds.
4. Add the eggplant and coat in the oil and spice mixture, sauté for about 2 minutes until starting to brown.
5. Pour the coconut milk into the pot and stir to combine.

6. Press the "soup" button on the Instant Pot and "adjust" the time to 5 minutes.

7. Secure the lid onto the Instant Pot and make sure the steam valve is closed.

8. Once the pot beeps, carefully depressurize and release the steam.

9. Remove the lid and add the fresh coriander to the pot.

10. Ladle the eggplant and coconut into bowls.

11. ENJOY!

Stuffed spaghetti squash (V)

Spaghetti squash can be hard to find in certain supermarkets, but if you can get your hands on one, grab it! They're very keto-friendly, and extremely yummy. This recipe has cheese, spices, spinach and cream.

Serves: 4

Ingredients:

- 1 spaghetti squash, cut in half, seeds removed
- 2tbsp olive oil
- 2 garlic cloves, crushed
- 1/2 tsp cinnamon
- ½ tsp chilli powder
- ½ tsp cumin
- 4 cups baby spinach
- ½ cup full-fat cream
- Salt and pepper
- 1 cup mozzarella, grated

Method:

1. Press the "sauté" button on your Instant Pot and keep the temperature at "normal".
2. Add the oil to the pot.
3. Once the oil is hot, add the garlic, cinnamon, chilli powder, and cumin, sauté for 30 seconds.
4. Add the spinach, stir until the spinach has wilted.
5. Add the cream to the pot and stir through, add salt and pepper.

6. Remove the creamy spinach mixture and keep to the side in a bowl.
7. Clean the pot out and add 1 cup of water to the clean pot.
8. Place the spaghetti squash halves into the basket which came with your Instant Pot.
9. Secure the lid onto the pot and make sure the steam valve is closed.
10. Press the "steam" button and "adjust" the time to 7 minutes.
11. Once the pot beeps, carefully depressurize the pot and remove the lid.
12. Take the spaghetti squash out of the basket and fill them with the spinach mixture.
13. Sprinkle the mozzarella on top of the filled spaghetti squash halves.
14. Place the filled halves under the grill in the oven to melt the cheese.
15. Scoop out the squash and spinach mixture just before serving.
16. ENJOY!

Leek, mushroom, and coconut stew (V, VG)

It's not really a stew, it's not really a soup...but I had to choose one so I called it a stew! Basically, this recipe combines the onion-y goodness of leeks, the delicate earthiness of mushrooms, and the creaminess of coconut milk. I guess you could call it a curry...but a lot milder. Go on, make it yourself and call it what you like!

Serves: 4

Ingredients:

- 2 large leeks, cut into thin strips
- 2 cups brown mushrooms, sliced (or any mushrooms you can get)
- 2tbsp olive oil
- 1 onion, finely chopped
- 2 garlic cloves, finely chopped
- 1tsp ground turmeric
- 1tsp ground cumin
- Small handful of coriander, finely chopped
- 1 can full-fat coconut milk (about 400ml)

Method:

1. Press the "sauté" button on your Instant Pot and keep the temperature at "normal".
2. Add the olive oil to the pot.
3. Once the oil is hot, add the garlic, onion, turmeric, and cumin to the pot, sauté until the onion is soft.
4. Add the leeks and mushrooms to the pot and stir to coat in oil and spices.

5. Add the coconut milk to the pot and secure the lid onto the pot, make sure the steam valve is closed.
6. Press the "soup" button and "adjust" the time to 5 minutes.
7. Carefully depressurize the pot and remove the lid.
8. Stir the mixture and serve while hot, with a sprinkling of fresh coriander.
9. ENJOY!

Broccoli, asparagus, pumpkin seed, and fresh mint salad (V, VG)

This salad offers so much green goodness, you'll feel revitalized after just one bowl. I love the addition of fresh mint, as it gives a fresh and invigorating taste.

Serves: 4

Ingredients:

- 1 head of broccoli, cut into florets
- 12 asparagus spears, cut in half (remove the woody ends first)
- Salt and pepper
- 2tbsp pumpkin seeds
- 1 small handful fresh mint leaves, finely chopped
- 2tbsp olive oil
- 1tbsp apple cider vinegar

Method:

1. Pour 1 cup of water into the Instant pot.
2. Place the broccoli and asparagus into the steaming basket which came with your Instant Pot, sprinkle with salt and pepper.
3. Secure the lid onto the Instant Pot, make sure the steam valve is closed.
4. Press the "steam" button and "adjust" the time to 3 minutes.
5. Once the pot beeps, carefully depressurize and remove the lid.

6. Place the asparagus and broccoli into a bowl and sprinkle the pumpkin seeds over.
7. Mix together the olive oil, apple cider vinegar, and fresh mint, pour over the vegetables and stir through.
8. Serve warm.
9. ENJOY!

Spinach, pecan, strawberry, and mozzarella salad (V)

This salad just screams "Summertime". Fresh, juicy strawberries burst with sweetness and match perfectly with the pecan nuts, mozzarella, and spinach. The only cooking you need to do in this recipe is lightly toasting the pecans, which the Instant Pot can take care of.

Serves: 4 – 6 (4 large servings, 6 smaller servings)

Ingredients:

- 5 cups baby spinach
- ¼ cup pecans, roughly chopped
- 12 large strawberries, cut into quarters
- 2 cups mozzarella, roughly torn or chopped
- 2tbsp olive oil or avocado oil
- 1tbsp apple cider vinegar
- Salt and pepper

Method:

1. Press the "sauté" button on your Instant Pot and keep the temperature at "normal".
2. Add the chopped pecans to the pot and stir to avoid burning, once they are lightly toasted and golden, remove them from the pot and let them cool.
3. In a large bowl, mix the spinach leaves, chopped strawberries, mozzarella, and pecans.
4. Mix together the olive or avocado oil, salt, pepper and apple cider vinegar, pour over the salad and gently toss.
5. ENJOY!

Spinach, feta, and ricotta balls (V)

These balls have not one, but TWO types of cheese. They kind of remind me of gnocchi, but without all the carbs. You can have these as a starter or light meal with any low-carb dip you like.

Serves: 4 (makes 16 balls)

Ingredients:

- 3 cups baby spinach leaves, finely chopped
- 200gm feta cheese, cut or crumbled into small pieces
- 250gm full-fat ricotta
- 1 egg
- Salt and pepper
- Zest of ½ lemon
- 2tbsp olive oil

Method:

1. In a medium bowl, mix together the spinach, ricotta, feta, salt, pepper, and lemon zest.
2. Press the "sauté" button on your Instant Pot and keep the temperature at "normal".
3. Pour the olive oil into the pot.
4. Once the oil is hot, roll balls of the cheesy spinach mixture, (don't worry if you can't make perfect ball shapes, they don't have to be perfect! If they crumble or slightly break apart, just shape them back together).
5. Place the balls into the hot oil, you might have to do 2 or 3 batches so the balls don't become crowded.
6. Cook the balls for about 5 minutes, turning them a few times to brown them all over.
7. Serve while warm.
8. ENJOY!

Zucchini and eggplant with fried almond crumb (V, VG)

This dish slightly resembles a lasagne in the sense that it is layered with tomato sauce. Instead of a cheesy sauce, the top is encrusted with a gorgeous, nutty crumb.

Serves: 4

Ingredients:

- 3-4 zucchinis, sliced lengthways
- 1 large eggplant, sliced
- 1 can chopped tomatoes
- 2 garlic cloves
- 2tbsp olive oil
- ¼ cup almonds roughly chopped, toasted
- ¼ cup ground almonds
- Salt and pepper

Method:

1. Press the "sauté" button on your Instant Pot and keep the temperature at "normal".
2. Place the chopped almonds and ground almonds in the pot and keep stirring while they toast, for about 2 minutes (or until golden but not burnt).
3. Take the almonds out of the pot and set aside.
4. Pour a drizzle of olive oil into the pot and heat for 30 seconds.
5. Add the garlic to the pot and sauté until soft.
6. Add the chopped tomatoes to the pot and stir through.

7. Once the tomatoes are hot, remove them from the pot and rinse the pot out.
8. In a small dish or steam-proof bowl, place a layer of zucchini slices, spoon over a small amount of tomatoes, then add a layer of eggplant slices, then more tomatoes, then another layer of zucchini slices. Keep layering in this fashion until all of the zucchini, eggplant, and tomatoes have been used.
9. Place a trivet into the instant pot and pour 1 cup of water into the bottom of the pot.
10. Place the eggplant dish on top of the trivet.
11. Press the "steam" button and "adjust" the time to 3 minutes.
12. Secure the lid onto the pot and make sure the steam valve is closed.
13. Once the pot beeps, allow the pot to depressurize on its own and then carefully remove the lid.
14. Take the dish out of the pot and sprinkle with the almond mixture and a sprinkling of salt and pepper.
15. Add a drizzle of olive oil over the top of the dish and eat while hot.
16. ENJOY!

Power-packed salad with boiled eggs, haloumi, and nut sprinkle (V)

There are a few salads in this section, because for me, they are one of the best ways to ensure a hefty dose of vegetables in one meal. You can add any low-carb ingredients you wish, but this recipe is one of my personal favourites, because I just love haloumi.

Serves: 4

Ingredients:

- 4 eggs, (hard boiled in the Instant Pot by steaming for 5 minutes, see the recipe in the "Breakfast" section), cut into quarters
- 2tbsp olive oil
- 250gm block of haloumi, sliced into 12 slices
- 1 head of iceberg lettuce, roughly chopped
- ½ cucumber, cut into small chunks
- 1 avocado, cut into chunks
- ¼ cup mixed nuts and seeds such as almonds, pecans, macadamias, sesame seeds, and pumpkin seeds
- 1tbsp apple cider vinegar
- Salt and pepper

Method:

1. Press the "sauté" button on your Instant Pot and keep the temperature at "normal".
2. Add the olive oil to the pot.

3. Once the oil is hot, add the haloumi slices and cook for 2 minutes, turn each piece over and cook the other side for 2 minutes, or until the haloumi is golden.
4. In a large bowl, combine the lettuce, cucumber, and avocado, pour over the apple cider vinegar and gently toss through.
5. Place the haloumi and eggs on top of the salad.
6. Sprinkle over the nut/seed mixture.
7. Serve in salad bowls with even amounts of egg and haloumi (or a few more haloumi slices for you...no one will know!).
8. ENJOY!

Stuffed green peppers with mushrooms and walnuts (V, VG)

There's something so great about stuffing vegetables, it makes them so much tastier and more interesting. Green peppers go really well with mushrooms and walnuts, as this recipe proves! For a non-vegan option, throw some feta cheese in there!

Serves: 4

Ingredients

4 green peppers, stalk and seeds removed (scoop them out and keep the pepper whole)
3 cups brown mushrooms, sliced
¼ cup walnuts, roughly chopped
Sprig of fresh thyme, roughly chopped
1tbsp olive oil
2 garlic cloves, finely chopped

Method:

1. Place the peppers in the basket which came with your Instant Pot, sprinkle with salt.
2. Pour 1 cup into the Instant Pot and place the basket of peppers into the pot.
3. Secure the lid onto the pot and make sure the steam valve is closed.
4. Press the "steam" button and "adjust" the time to 3 minutes.
5. Once the pot beeps, carefully depressurize the pot and remove the lid.
6. Remove the basket and leave the peppers to cool.
7. Tip out the water from the pot.

8. Press the "sauté" button and keep the temperature at "normal".
9. Add the olive oil to the pot.
10. Once the oil is hot, add the garlic and thyme, sauté for 20 seconds but don't burn the garlic.
11. Add the mushrooms and sauté until soft.
12. Add the walnuts and stir through.
13. Stuff the cooked peppers with mushroom and walnut mixture.
14. Return the peppers to the pot to sauté the bottoms for about 1 minute.
15. Serve while hot.
16. ENJOY!

Olive, caper, and anchovy "pasta" (V, VG)

Olives, capers and anchovies are some of my favourite ingredients, as they feature in one of my favourite classic Italian dishes "puttanesca". This dish leaves out the tomato. Get your spiralizer ready to go!

Serves: 4

Ingredients:

- 5 large zucchinis, "spiralized" or thinly peeled with a peeler
- 2tbsp olive oil
- 5 anchovies
- 3 garlic cloves, finely chopped
- 2tbsp capers
- ¼ cup chopped black olives
- Grated parmesan cheese to serve

Method:

1. Press the "sauté" button on your Instant Pot and keep the temperature at "normal".
2. Add the olive oil to the pot.
3. Once the oil is hot, add the garlic and anchovies to the put and break up the anchovies with a wooden spoon.
4. Add the capers, olives, and zucchini.
5. Sauté the mixture for 5 minutes, or until the zucchini is soft according to your liking (I like mine to be have a crunch).
6. Serve while hot, with a sprinkling of grated cheese on top.
7. ENJOY!

Cabbage and cauliflower fried "rice" (V, VG option)

A big bowl of fried rice never goes out of fashion in my house. The great thing about Keto is that you CAN have a BIG bowl of fried rice...because it's not really rice! This cabbage and cauliflower fried rice is incredibly moreish. If you are vegan, then simply leave off the egg on top!

Serves: 4-6 (4 large serves, 6 medium serves)

Ingredients:

- 1 large cauliflower head, blitzed in the blender to resemble rice
- Half a head of cabbage (green cabbage), cut into thin slices
- 3 garlic cloves, finely chopped
- 1 onion, finely chopped
- 1 carrot, chopped into small cubes
- 3tbsp coconut oil
- 3tbsp soy sauce
- 2tsp chilli flakes
- Eggs, 1 per person (unless vegan), fried or poached to your liking

Method:

1. Press the "sauté" button on your Instant Pot and keep the temperature at "normal".
2. Add the coconut oil to the pot.
3. When the coconut oil is melted, add the onion, garlic, and carrot, sauté until the onion is soft.

4. Add the cabbage and cauliflower and stir to coat in coconut oil.
5. Sauté the cabbage and cauliflower until both are soft.
6. Add the soy sauce and chilli flakes and stir through.
7. Once the vegetables are at your desired softness, (I like mine slightly charred) remove from the pot and serve with an egg on top.
8. ENJOY!

Sides

Side dishes are a great way of adding extra vegetables and healthy fats to your diet. What's more, side dishes give you more options to satisfy multiple cravings in one meal! Some of these recipes are fresh and zingy, such as the "Asian greens with garlic and chilli". There are also some extremely creamy and decadent sides in this collection, such as "Creamy mushrooms" which can be used as a sauce on steak, or with eggs and bacon at breakfast time.

Chicken nibbles with garlic, soy, and sesame seeds

This is more of a party food than it is a "side", but I thought it was best fitted for this section, as sometimes I like to cook up a bunch of these to have on the side of a soup or vegetable dish.

Serves: about 6 as a starter or side dish

Ingredients:

- 2lb chicken nibbles
- 3 garlic cloves, crushed
- 3tbsp soy sauce
- 3tbsp olive oil
- 3tbsp sesame seeds, lightly toasted

Method:

1. Combine garlic, soy sauce, and olive oil in a large bowl.
2. Add the chicken nibbles to the bowl and coat them in the sauce.

3. Press the "sauté" button on your Instant Pot, and keep the temperature at "normal".
4. Once the pot is hot, add the chicken nibbles and sauce, sauté for 3 minutes.
5. Press the "poultry" button on your instant pot and "adjust" the time to 8 minutes.
6. Secure the lid onto the Instant Pot and make sure the steam valve is closed.
7. Once the pot beeps, carefully depressurize the pot and remove the lid.
8. Sprinkle the chicken nibbles with the toasted sesame seeds and stir to coat.
9. Remove the chicken nibbles and place them in a large serving bowl.
10. ENJOY!

Keto mac and cheese

I have added this mac and cheese recipe to the "sides" section because it's great as a fat-filled side for meat or vegetable dishes. However, if you are craving a super-rich, satisfying main dish, then go ahead and have a full serving of this gooey deliciousness! There is no thickening agent in this mac and cheese recipe, so the sauce is a little runnier than usual, but I think it's better that way!

Serves: 6 small servings as a starter

Ingredients:

- 1 large cauliflower head, cut into small pieces, about the size of macaroni
- 4tbsp butter
- Salt and pepper
- 2 garlic cloves, finely chopped
- 1 cup full-fat cream
- 1 cup sharp cheddar cheese, grated
- ½ cup mozzarella, grated

Method:

1. Place the cauliflower in your steamer bowl (or the basket which came with your Instant Pot).
2. Pour ½ cup water into the Instant Pot and place the basket of cauliflower into the pot.
3. Press the "steam" button on your Instant Pot and "adjust" the time to 1 minute.
4. Secure the lid onto the pot and make sure the steam valve is closed.

5. Once the pot beeps, safely depressurize the pot and remove the lid.
6. Remove the cauliflower and discard the water in the pot.
7. Press the "sauté" button on your Instant Pot and "adjust" the temperature to "normal".
8. Add the butter to the pot.
9. Once the butter is melted, add the garlic and cook for 30 seconds.
10. Add the cream and both cheeses to the pot, keep stirring.
11. Keep stirring the mixture until the cheese is melted and the sauce has become thick.
12. Add the cauliflower to the pot and stir through the sauce.
13. Sprinkle with salt and pepper, stir through.
14. Serve while hot.
15. ENJOY!

Kale chips

To be honest, I ate kale chips all the time even when I wasn't doing Keto! They are so satisfyingly crunchy, salty, and moreish. I like to add chilli flakes to mine, because I LOVE chilli, but you can leave it out if you prefer!

Serves: 1 medium bowl of kale chips (serves about 2 or 3 people as a light snack)

Ingredients:

- 1 bag of kale, (about 10 large leaves), washed, dried and torn into "chip-sized" pieces
- 2tbsp olive oil
- Salt
- Chilli flakes

Method:

1. Press the "sauté" button on your Instant Pot and adjust the temperature to "less".
2. Pour the olive oil into the pot.
3. Once the oil is hot, add the kale to the pot in batches so that the kale sits in a single layer in the pot.
4. Sprinkle each layer with salt and chilli as it sits in the pot.
5. Watch the kale as they gently fry, turning them over once.
6. Once the kale has "dried out" and become crunchy, remove it with a slotted spoon and place it in a bowl.
7. ENJOY!

Buttery Brussels sprouts (JUST TRY THEM!)

I know, I know, Brussels sprouts have a terrible reputation. But, if you haven't tried them in a while, give them another chance! They can be so delicious when cooked in the right way. I have included them in the "sides" section, as they should be eaten moderately in order to ensure ketosis. I eat about 4- 5 of them per sitting, and it's completely fine.

Serves: 3 (5 sprouts each)

Ingredients:

- 15 Brussels sprouts, cut in half
- Salt and Pepper
- 2tbsp olive oil
- 2tbsp butter
- 2 garlic cloves, finely chopped
- 1tbsp chilli flakes (optional)
- Water

Method:

1. Place the sprouts in a metal steaming bowl, (or the basket your Instant Pot came with) and sprinkle them with salt and pepper.
2. Pour ½ cup water into the instant pot, place the basket with the sprouts into the pot.
3. Press the "steam" button on your Instant Pot and "adjust" the time to 2 minutes.
4. Once the pot beeps, carefully release the steam, and remove the lid.

5. Remove the basket of sprouts and tip the water out of the Instant Pot.
6. Press the "sauté" button on the Instant Pot and keep the temperature at "normal".
7. Pour the olive oil and butter into the pot.
8. Once the butter is melted, add the garlic and heat for about 30 seconds.
9. Add the Brussels sprouts and coat them in the oil and butter.
10. Cook the Brussels sprouts in the Instant Pot until they become brown and almost charred and sticky.
11. Remove the sprouts and place them in a serving bowl.
12. Sprinkle over the optional chilli.
13. ENJOY!

Bacon, mozzarella, and spinach bundles

These bundles are so yummy, and adorably cute, you might just end up eating them as your main dish! Bacon and mozzarella are obviously a delicious pairing, but I had to have some greenery in there, and spinach was the perfect choice.

Serves: makes about 12 bundles (3 per person...if you can resist)

Ingredients:

- 250gm mozzarella, cut into 12 even pieces
- 12 rashers of streaky bacon
- A large handful of baby spinach leaves
- Olive oil

Method:

1. Wrap each piece of mozzarella in spinach, about 4 leaves per piece.
2. Wrap each spinach-coated piece of mozzarella with a rasher of bacon, make sure you wrap them tightly so the spinach is covered.
3. The bundles should now look like round, bacon-covered balls.
4. Press the "sauté" button on your Instant Pot and keep the temperature at "normal".
5. Drizzle the olive oil into the pot.
6. Once the oil is hot, add the bundles to the pot in groups of 6.
7. Cook for about 3 minutes, then turn the bundles over and cook the other side for another 3 minutes or until golden and sizzling.
8. Serve while hot...the cheese will be melted inside.
9. ENJOY!

Garlic butter green beans and broccoli rabe with slivered almonds

A heaping bowl of buttery greens is a heavenly accompaniment to any dish. Green beans and broccoli rabe are great partners, and they will brighten up any dish. Slivered almonds add a touch of class, and a sprinkling of crunch.

Serves: 4 as a starter or side

Ingredients:

- 2 cups frozen green beans
- 2-3 stems of broccoli rabe per person
- 2tbsp slivered almonds
- 2 garlic cloves, finely chopped
- 2tbsp butter
- 1tbsp olive oil

Method:

1. Press the "sauté" button on your Instant Pot and keep the temperature at "normal".
2. Add the butter and olive oil to the pot and heat until the butter is melted.
3. Add the garlic to the pot and heat until soft.
4. Add the beans and broccoli rabe and stir until coated with the oil and butter.
5. Sauté for about 5 minutes or until the beans are cooked through.
6. Place on a plate, or in a serving bowl, and sprinkle with the slivered almonds.
7. ENJOY!

Creamy mushrooms

I LOVE creamy mushrooms! The warm, earthy, slightly sweet flavour is such a great accompaniment to meat dishes. Add this delicious side to your morning eggs and bacon for a super dose of healthy fats and vegetables.

Serves: 4 sides

Ingredients:

- 3 cups sliced mushrooms – all kinds of mushrooms are fine, but I like Portobello
- 2 garlic cloves, finely chopped
- 1tbsp olive oil
- 1 knob of butter (about 2tsp but no need to be too precise)
- 1/2tsp dried thyme
- 150ml heavy cream

Method:

1. Press the "sauté" button on your Instant Pot and keep the temperature at "normal".
2. Add the olive oil and butter to the pot, heat until butter is melted.
3. Add the garlic and dried herbs to the pot and heat until soft.
4. Add the mushrooms to the pot and stir through until the mushrooms are coated with oil and butter.
5. Add the cream and stir until combined.
6. Keep an eye on the pot and stir occasionally, until the mushrooms are soft and the cream is thick.
7. Serve any way you like!
8. ENJOY!

Parmesan and pecan-crusted zucchini fries

Parmesan and pecans are a great combination when you want to mimic breadcrumbs. The parmesan offers a sharp creaminess, and the pecans are nutty and crunchy. Yes, we are turning to the wonderful zucchini again! This time, the zucchini is cut into thick "fries" and fried in olive oil. Serve with guacamole, herb-garlic yogurt, or the queso dip recipe below!

Serves: approximately 4 people as a side or starter

Ingredients:

- 3-4 medium zucchinis, cut into thick fries
- 3oz parmesan cheese, finely grated
- ¼ cup pecans, finely chopped
- 1 garlic clove, finely chopped
- 2 eggs, lightly beaten
- 4tbsp olive oil

Method:

1. Mix together parmesan, pecans, and a pinch of salt and pepper in a bowl.
2. Dip each zucchini piece in the beaten egg until coated.
3. Roll the egg-coated zucchini in the parmesan-pecan mixture until coated.
4. Place zucchini on a plate while you complete the following steps.
5. Press the "Sauté" button on the Instant Pot and "adjust" the temperature to "more".
6. Add the olive oil and heat for about 20 seconds.

7. Once the oil is heated, place the zucchini into the bottom of the pot in a single layer.
8. Fry for about 2 minutes, and then turn over to fry the other side.
9. Remove the zucchini once each side is golden brown.
10. Place onto a plate with a paper-towel to soak up the excess oil.
11. Serve with any dip you like! (Keto, of course!).
12. ENJOY!

Queso dip

Come on, who doesn't like delicious melted cheese? (Vegans, avert your eyes!). This dip is so delicious you'll have to serve it to a group of people, otherwise you WILL eat it all yourself. Dip celery sticks and cucumber into this golden, heavenly concoction for a fresh-but-luxurious starter. Be sure to attend the pot and keep stirring so it doesn't catch and burn.

Serves: one medium-sized serving bowl of dip (a starter for 4-5 people)

Ingredients:

- 7ounces of cheese – you can use a mixture, I recommend sharp cheddar and blue, grated
- 80ml heavy cream
- 1tsp paprika
- 1 garlic clove, crushed
- 1tbsp olive oil
- Pickled jalapenos, chopped, use as many as you like, depending on taste, I use about 3tbsp

Method:

1. Press the "sauté" button on your Instant Pot and "adjust" the temperature to "low".
2. Add the oil and heat for about 10 seconds.
3. Add the garlic, paprika, and chopped jalapenos and coat them in the oil.
4. Add the cheese and cream to the pot.

5. Combine all of the ingredients until it's all incorporated.
6. Keep stirring until the cheese is melted and hot.
7. Either serve in the pot (just remove the inner pot) or spoon the dip into a bowl.
8. Serve with low-carb veggie sticks such as cucumber, green pepper, or celery.
9. ENJOY!

Asian greens with garlic and chilli

Asian greens such as Bok choy are very low-carb, and full of fantastic nutrients. They are a great side dish for all kinds of dishes, and can be glammed-up with all kinds of flavours. This recipe uses garlic and chilli to really ramp-up the flavour profile. A couple of drops of sesame oil drizzled on top before serving gives a delicious, nutty flavour. You can use any Asian greens you like, I recommend Pak Choi, Bok Choi, or Shanghai Bok Choi. For steaming, you will need a stainless-steel basket to place the vegetables in.

Serves: 4 servings of Asian greens (or one huge one if you're up for it)

Ingredients:

- 4 whole heads of Asian greens
- 1tbsp coconut oil
- 1 cup water
- 2 garlic cloves, finely chopped
- ½ a fresh red chilli, finely chopped (deseeded if you don't want it to be too spicy)
- ½ tsp sesame oil

Method:

1. Place a stainless-steel basket into the Instant Pot and put the Asian greens in it.
2. Pour the water over the greens so it drains into the bottom of the Instant Pot.
3. Secure the lid onto the Instant Pot and turn the steam vent to "pressure" (so the steam doesn't escape).

4. Press the "steam" button and manually change the time by pressing the "minus" button until the digital window shows 1 minute.

5. While the vegetables are steaming, place coconut oil, garlic, and chilli in a small frying pan and sauté until soft.

6. When the Instant Pot timer beeps, carefully open the steam vent manually, to let the steam out and prevent the greens from becoming soggy.

7. Place the greens on a plate.

8. Pour over the garlic and chilli mixture.

9. Drizzle the sesame oil over the top.

10. ENJOY!

Creamed spinach

It's no secret that spinach is one of the most nutritious foods on the planet. On its own, it can be a bit bland and boring (it is for me anyway!). But as soon as you add cream and garlic, it's a total game changer. This creamy spinach dish can be served on the side of any dish you like, and it is also fantastic on top of steak as a sauce.

Serves: 4 side servings

Ingredients:

- One whole bag of baby spinach (about 8 cups, it wilts!)
- Drizzle of olive oil (about 1tbsp)
- 2 garlic cloves, finely chopped
- 100ml heavy cream

Method:

1. Press the "sauté" button on your Instant Pot and keep the temperature at "normal".
2. Add the olive oil and heat for about 10 seconds.
3. Add the garlic and sauté until soft but not burnt.
4. Add the spinach and stir into the garlic and oil until wilted.
5. Add the cream and stir through, with a sprinkle of salt and pepper.
6. Keep stirring until the cream thickens and the spinach is soft and completed wilted.
7. Serve as a side to any meat or vegetable dishes.
8. ENJOY!

Cauliflower mash

Cauliflower is a fantastic alternative to many starchy foods such as bread (cauliflower pizza base, anyone?), rice, and potato. This recipe mimics the comfort of mashed potato, with a fraction of the carbs. The butter and cream adds a nice hit of fat and decadence. This is a great side for Winter stews and casseroles...or with just about anything! It's kind of like the little sister to the creamy cauliflower soup recipe earlier in this recipe book.

Serves: 4

Ingredients:

- 1 cauliflower head (it doesn't matter if it's slightly smaller or larger than average, the quantities still work) chopped into small pieces
- 30 grams of butter
- 3tbsp heavy cream
- A pinch of chilli powder or dried chilli flakes (optional, but add it in if you love a kick of heat!)

Method:

1. Place a rack or basket in the Instant Pot.
2. Place the chopped cauliflower on/in the rack or basket.
3. Sprinkle the cauliflower with salt.
4. Secure the lid into the Instant Pot.
5. Press the "Steam" function button.
6. Press the "adjust" button and then the "less" button until the time is set for 3 minutes.

7. Walk away and let the Instant Pot do its magic and gently soften your cauliflower.
8. Once the pot has depressurized on its own, remove the lid carefully.
9. Tip the cauliflower into a bowl and add the butter, cream, and some cracked pepper.
10. Mash the mixture together with a potato masher, the butter will melt into the hot cauliflower.
11. Serve, and as usual...ENJOY!

Sautéed asparagus with crispy bacon

Who doesn't like bacon?! Well, vegetarians of course...but Vegans and Vege's can still make this dish, just leave out the bacon! Asparagus is a great vegetable when it's in season, so make the most of it when you can! Some people have an aversion to asparagus because it can be cooked to smithereens and is not so appetizing when it's slimy and mushy. However, if you sauté it, like this recipe advises, then it becomes a crunchy and delicious treat you will LOVE. Go on, give it a chance!

Serves: 4

Ingredients:

- 16 spears of asparagus (4 per person)
- 4 rashers of streaky bacon
- Small knob of butter
- One small garlic clove, crushed

Method:

1. Press the "Sauté" button on your Instant Pot and adjust the temperature setting to "normal".
2. Add the butter and heat till melted.
3. Add the crushed garlic and heat gently, careful not to burn.
4. Add the pieces of bacon and sauté till slightly crispy (or very crispy, depending how you like it!).
5. Add the asparagus and toss through the bacon and garlic mixture so each spear is coated.
6. Sauté asparagus until it is slightly tender but still has a crunch to it.
7. Remove from the Instant Pot and serve on a side-plate with a few grinds of salt and pepper to taste.
8. ENJOY!

Conclusion

Hopefully you now feel ready to embark on your Ketogenic journey, or to carry on bravely if you've already started. Whether your goal is to lose weight, have more energy, or simply get into some clean-eating habits, the Ketogenic Diet is the perfect place to start.

The rules and restrictions don't need to be cumbersome or boring if you are prepared and you have all the right information at hand. Make sure you have a list of "good" foods and "bad" foods somewhere visible in your kitchen, so when you are preparing your meals, you can easily check if you're on the Keto route. Having a fridge and freezer full of vegetables and meat will help you to create fast and easy dishes when you need them.

If you are just starting Keto, remember to drink lots of water and add some salt to your meals when you first start your Keto diet, to ward off any side effects. If you still don't feel back to normal after a week, then check with your doctor!

If you don't already have an Instant Pot, I highly recommend it, especially if you have a busy life. As you will see from these recipes, the Instant Pot allows you to cook quickly, efficiently, and safely. Slow cooked meat and soups can be especially time-consuming, so if you're a fan of these kinds of dishes, then the Instant Pot is definitely for you!

Good luck!

Helpful Keto resources I have learned from and turned to for advice

https://www.ruled.me/the-ketogenic-diet-and-cholesterol/

https://mhunters.com/en/blog/burn-lose-stubborn-belly-fat-ketosis/

https://www.perfectketo.com/ketosis-side-effects/

http://lowcarbediem.com/have-more-energy-sleep-less-and-get-more-done/

http://www.healthline.com/nutrition/ketogenic-diet-101#section2

https://www.ruled.me/guide-keto-diet/#dangers-of-keto

https://ketodietapp.com/Blog/post/2015/01/03/Keto-Diet-Food-List-What-to-Eat-and-Avoid

https://ketodietapp.com/Blog/post/2015/09/13/how-to-exercise-on-a-keto-diet

https://www.news-medical.net/health/History-of-the-Ketogenic-Diet.aspx

http://www.seriouseats.com/2016/01/best-cut-beef-stew-braise.html

Made in the USA
Lexington, KY
20 November 2017